INTRODUCTION

Since the pages of this book was digitized from a very old original,
the pages here may look a little funny at times.
Rest assured we did our best to format the original book
into modern form as best allowed by the current processes available.

Ross Brown

Introduction and Cover Art Copyright 2009 -
All rights reserved.
SoHoBooks
ISBN 1441435705

For regular updates on new reprint editions of
vintage cookbooks,
vintage cocktail books,
vintage bartender books
vintage drink books and
vintage wine books
please visit

www.HistoricCookbooks.com

Sunkist Recipes
Oranges-Lemons

Tested and Compiled by
MISS ALICE BRADLEY
Principal of
Miss Farmer's School of Cookery
BOSTON, MASS.

**The Fruit of a Hundred Uses
Buy Them by the Box**

Sunkist Recipes

A Word to Housewives
By Miss Bradley

THE recipes in this book were prepared for women who like oranges and lemons and who have learned that there is a wide difference between ordinary oranges and lemons and the *selected* fruit from California, which is sold by first-class dealers throughout the country under the name "Sunkist."

It is interesting to learn why Sunkist Oranges are so good—why they are as fresh, luscious and superbly flavored when they reach your table as if you had stepped out into your own yard and picked them from the tree.

Sunkist Oranges grow in California, and only California sunshine and soil can produce the flavor and quality you get in Sunkist Oranges.

These oranges are picked every day in the year and shipped, fresh, to all parts of the country.

This golden fruit is grown, gathered and shipped by over

Sunkist Recipes

8,000 progressive growers, who have co-operated to form the California Fruit Growers Exchange, a wonderful organization, which will be described later in this book.

Now, just a word about the healthfulness of oranges.

If every person would eat one Sunkist Orange a day, he or she would find the resulting benefit really surprising. Increase this number to two or three, and the benefits will be correspondingly multiplied, for this rich, sweet juice is one of Nature's most potent tonics and alteratives.

A pure, live fruit juice, such as oranges afford, should be given liberally to children. Remember, that doctors put orange juice on the diet list of little babies.

* * * *

Sunkist Oranges peel easily, and the segments may then be separated and eaten from the fingers. When pared with a sharp knife the inner membrane can be removed with the peel, leaving a juicy, brilliantly-colored meat, which may either be sliced or taken out in sections and freed from membrane.

* * * *

Sunkist Lemons are superior in acidity, flavor, appearance, and general quality. The price is the same as you must pay for ordinary lemons. Therefore, you should insist on seeing the Sunkist wrapper when you order your lemons.

Sunkist Lemons are waxy and bright, practically seedless; therefore, easily sliced without marring, making them an ideal lemon for garnishing.

The value of diluted lemon juice is well appreciated by physicians. It may be taken in cold or hot water, plain or sweetened, to advantage. It clears the throat, sweetens the breath, keeps the gums in a healthy condition, and is excellent for internal disorders, such as biliousness.

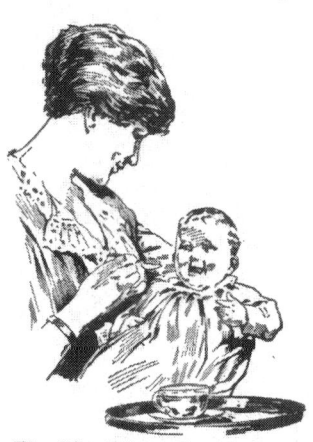

The Ideal Diet For Babies

Sunkist Recipes

The use of lemon juice to remove kitchen stains from the hands makes a lemon an indispensable article of the toilet. Lemon juice is also valuable in cleaning brass and copper, and in whitening a scoured table or sink. Lemon juice and milk, generously applied to ink stains on white goods, will remove the stains completely.

In pressing the juice from Sunkist Lemons and Oranges, the glass or china squeezers are best and most convenient. The best orangeade is undiluted Sunkist Orange Juice, served in thin glasses, one-third full of cracked ice. For young children, strain the Sunkist Orange Juice through a fine wire strainer or through cheesecloth, and serve in a thick punch-glass.

When recipes call for grated rind of Sunkist Oranges or Lemons, it is important that care be taken to remove only the yellow portion. The white portion of the skin of oranges and lemons is rich in pectin, the substance that causes fruit juices to jell when boiled with sugar. An extraction of this pectin can be added to the juice of strawberries and other fruits, making a firm jelly of what would, otherwise, be only a thick syrup.

Orange and Lemon baskets, shells and cups can be used for serving mixtures. The meat of the fruit should be removed with a teaspoon, and the edges cut with a sharp knife, scissors, or one of the patent cutters. Other methods of cutting lemons for garnishing may be seen in the illustrations. The tub with two handles, filled with Lemon Butter, holds a "tree" of watercress. Sliced lemon, in the case, is made of the peel, cut down in long strips. Sections may easily be re-

Sunkist Orange Juice Extractor

Sunkist Recipes

moved from the "pig" when lemon juice is needed on a piece of fish. Chopped parsley, paprika and small pieces of pimento decorate the notched halves of lemon, the slices and sections. A notched slice of lemon with a flower thrust through it is a pretty garnish in the fingerbowl.

Oranges and lemons are at their best and most beneficial when uncooked, and there are numberless ways of thus using them in the daily menu. They should also be kept on hand to add to the variety of the table by using them in made dishes, as few dishes, of any kind, are complete without a little lemon juice; or, may not be improved by the use of an orange.

Alice Bradley

Sunkist Recipes

Sunkist
Uniformly Good Oranges and Lemons

TWO things about oranges and lemons should be emphasized:

First, they are very healthful fruits—to which fact your physician will testify.

Second, California oranges are a *fresh fruit the year round*. They are picked from the trees in California every day throughout the year, and are shipped by fast freight to all the markets of the land. They come to you sealed in Nature's germproof package. They are ripened on the trees, and you can get them fresh every month of the year. Some people are surprised to learn this fact about Sunkist Oranges. It is a very important fact to the thousands of housewives who realize the advantage of *fresh, live* fruit, not only from the standpoint of *flavor*, but also of *healthfulness*.

Sunkist Recipes

Sunkist Oranges and Lemons together, as this book proves, lend themselves to scores of attractive recipes and household uses.

There are two principal kinds of Sunkist Oranges from California—the Sunkist Seedless Navel and the Sunkist Valencia Orange.

Sunkist Seedless Navel Oranges

The Sunkist Navel Orange is distinguished from the Sunkist Valencia by the navel formation at one end, and further, by the fact that the navel orange is *seedless*. Sunkist Navels are on the market in the Winter and Spring.

The meat of the Navel Orange is tender, but firm, and is bountifully supplied with a rich, full-bodied juice. This firm *tenderness*, which is a quality of the Valencia as well as the Navel, makes *any Sunkist Orange* ideal for slicing, segmenting, or cutting into small bits, for salads, desserts, etc.

Sunkist Valencia Oranges

Sunkist Valencia Oranges, as stated above, are firm, tender and juicy, like Navel Oranges, lending themselves just as readily to recipes. The Sunkist Valencia is an "*almost* seedless" orange; only a few seeds being found in this type. Sunkist Valencias are on the market in the Summer and Fall months.

Sunkist Lemons

California Sunkist Lemons are *practically seedless*. They are particularly desirable because of their juiciness, their tart, full-bodied flavor, and the fact that they are picked, packed and shipped under the most cleanly conditions.

Every Sunkist Citrus Fruit is picked by gloved hands, thoroughly cleansed with mechanical washers, and wrapped in clean tissue. *Sunkist Oranges and Lemons will be delivered to you in the original wrappers if you request it of your dealers.*

Sunkist Recipes

Another Important Fact

The California Fruit Growers Exchange, through which is shipped all citrus fruits bearing the Sunkist trademark, is a co-operative organization of more than 8,000 California citrus fruit-growers, who annually produce 30,000 carloads of oranges and lemons. It accumulates *no profits* and declares *no dividends*. Its purpose is to develop better methods of growing, picking, packing and shipping citrus fruits, and to distribute them with the greatest economy, so that these healthful fruits may be available at reasonable prices.

"Sunkist" is the trademark of the California Fruit Growers Exchange, and the oranges and lemons packed under it are carefully selected. They may be obtained in several different sizes. Housewives can *depend* on the fruit marked Sunkist, and it is therefore important to insist on "Sunkist Oranges" and "Sunkist Lemons" rather than to order merely "oranges" and "lemons."

All recipes in this book were compiled and tested by Miss Alice Bradley, Principal of Miss Farmer's School of Cookery, Boston, and are therefore authentic and reliable.

California Fruit Growers Exchange

A Co-operative Non-Profit Organization of 8,000 Growers

Los Angeles, California

Sunkist Recipes

Oranges For Health

Dr. Harvey W. Wiley Says They Are Better Than Medicine

Washington, July 8.—Doctor Harvey W. Wiley, former Chief of the Bureau of Chemistry of the Department of Agriculture, and universally admitted to be one of the greatest authorities on pure foods and dietetics in the world, says: "Eat oranges; eat them in Winter, eat them in Summer; eat as many as you can afford to buy; they are better for you than physic."

In an interview, Dr. Wiley says: "Oranges are excellent for people. It is good to eat oranges for breakfast, and also for dinner—not from a medical, but an antimedical standpoint. Both oranges and lemons ought to be used as freely as the financial ability of the consumer may permit. A laboring man may not be able always to

Sunkist Recipes

eat oranges at breakfast, yet the fruit is usually very cheap, and the consumption of it will obviate the need of physic and save many a doctor's bill.

"Note, that I do not say 'eat an orange for breakfast,' but rather 'EAT ORANGES.' Even if in straitened circumstances, people should eat plenty of oranges and lemons, not only in the Summertime, but all the time. I don't think anything I have ever said in praise of a fruit diet is too strong to say about oranges and lemons. The abundant production of oranges and lemons in California, their excellent quality, and the cheap transportation across the country, have put these blessings to mankind within the reach of every person of moderate circumstances.

"People ask, sometimes, whether oranges should be eaten at the beginning or end of a meal. It is better to eat oranges first; the effect cannot be so good after one has partaken of other food."

Mineral Contents of California Oranges and Lemons

	Navel Oranges	Cal. Lemons
Potash	30.18	40.63
Soda	1.54	1.47
Lime	14.00	25.20
Magnesia	3.29	3.80
Iron	0.60	0.35
Manganese	0.25	0.23
Phosphorus	7.52	9.30
Sulphur	3.23	2.39
Silica	0.40	0.55
Chlorine	0.57	0.33
Total Mineral	61.58	84.25

Sunkist Recipes

To Remove Pulp From Sunkist Oranges

Pare the orange with a sharp knife, removing every particle of the thin inside membrane with the peel. This will leave the orange pulp exposed. Hold the orange over a plate, so that any juice which may drop will be saved. Insert the point of the knife at the stem end of the orange, close to the membrane that divides the sections. Carefully work the knife in, separating the membrane from the section. Then carefully separate the section of orange from the membrane on its other side; remove the whole orange section, complete in shape, and entirely free from membrane. Repeat until all the sections are removed.

* * * *

NOTE:—In these recipes all measurements are made level. Measuring-cups, divided into thirds and quarters, are used, and tea and table measuring-spoons. Cups of dry material are filled to overflowing, by putting the material into the cup with a tablespoon, and are then leveled off with a knife. Tea and tablespoons are filled heaping with dry material, and then leveled off with a knife.

Most of the recipes in this book are proportioned to serve four people.

Sunkist Recipes

Dinner
*Meats and Fish Sauces-Relishes
Jellies-Vegetables
Breads and Sandwiches*

Oysters, with Cocktail Sauce

*24 oysters on half-shell
3 tablespoons Sunkist lemon juice
2 tablespoons tomato catsup
1 tablespoon finely-chopped onion
12 drops Tabasco sauce
½ teaspoon grated horseradish
Salt
4 Sunkist lemons*

Cut two sections from each Sunkist lemon; remove juice and pulp, leaving baskets with handles. Mix lemon juice with other seasonings, adding salt to taste. Put mixture in baskets, and place each one in centre of a deep plate of crushed ice. Arrange six oysters around each basket, and serve for a first course.

Oysters on the Half-Shell

Leave oysters on deep halves of shells, allowing six to each person. Place on plates of crushed ice, with small ends towards the centre; and where they meet, place a half of a Sunkist lemon, cut in points and sprinkled with a few grains of paprika.

Scallop Cocktail

Clean scallops; put in saucepan, and cook until they begin to shrivel. Drain, chill, and put in small scallop-shells, allowing two shells and ten scallops for each person. Arrange on plates of crushed ice, with lemon baskets in centre, filled with cocktail sauce, same as for oyster cocktail.

Sunkist Recipes

Little Neck Clams

Serve raw, like oysters, on the half-shell.

Lobster Cocktail

1 cup lobster meat
½ cup tomato catsup
2 teaspoons Worcestershire sauce
¼ cup Sunkist lemon juice
½ teaspoon Tabasco sauce
½ teaspoon finely-chopped chives
Salt to taste

Mix ingredients; salt to taste; chill thoroughly, and serve in cocktail glasses.

Mackerel, with Lemon Butter

Split and bone mackerel, and wipe with cheesecloth. Broil, first on flesh side, and then on the skin side, over a bed of hot coals or under the gas flame. Make six triangular slices of toast, and spread with lemon butter. Cut fish, and arrange pieces on the toast. Garnish with slices of Sunkist lemon and watercress.

Boiled Fish

A small whole fish, like cod or haddock, or a thick piece cut from a large fish, as salmon or halibut, may be used for boiling. Remove head and scales, and wipe with a piece of wet cheesecloth. In a kettle, or saucepan, put ingredients as for Court Bouillon (see page 17), and when it boils, add the fish. Cook just below boiling point until flesh leaves the bone, which will take from twenty to thirty minutes, depending on the size of the fish. Lift from the water, draining thoroughly; put on platter, and remove the skin. Pour over it Egg Sauce, or Hollandaise Sauce, and garnish with slices of Sunkist lemon and parsley. In serving, remove flesh carefully, leaving bones on the platter. The lemon juice in Court Bouillon helps to keep the fish white.

Fillets of Haddock, Lemon Sauce

1 small haddock
5 tablespoons butter
1 cup water
2 tablespoons Sunkist lemon juice
2 slices onion
2 tablespoons flour
¼ cup cream
1 egg yolk
Salt
Pepper

Skin and bone the haddock, and put in buttered pan; cover with

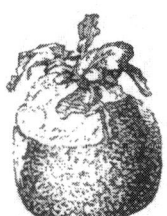 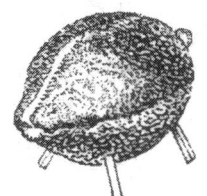 

Sunkist Lemon Garnishings

Sunkist Recipes

three tablespoons melted butter, and pour around the water, to which has been added the Sunkist lemon juice and onion. Cover and bake twenty-five minutes. Melt two tablespoons butter; add the flour, and, when smooth, the liquor from the pan, and stir until it boils. Beat egg yolk slightly; add cream, and stir into the sauce, just before serving. Season with salt and pepper; strain over fish, and garnish with parsley and lemon.

Salmon Chartreuse

Boiled salmon
2 tablespoons gelatine
½ cup cold water
1 tablespoon chopped carrot
1 tablespoon chopped onion
1 bay leaf
2 tablespoons chopped celery
Juice 1 Sunkist lemon
½ teaspoon salt
Few grains cayenne
2 cups water

Soak gelatine in one-half cup cold water. Put carrot, onion, celery and small bay leaf in two cups cold water; bring to boiling point; boil four minutes; add dissolved gelatine; strain; add lemon juice, salt and cayenne. Put a layer of this in the bottom of the mold; when firm, cover with pieces of cold boiled salmon (or, put on top of it, after gelatine has stiffened, a whole slice of boiled salmon), and pour over the remaining portion of the gelatine. Canned salmon may be used if fresh salmon is not at hand. When gelatine has stiffened, unmold on bed of lettuce leaves, and serve with mayonnaise dressing, or a sauce tartare, or green mayonnaise, made by coloring ordinary mayonnaise with parsley rubbed to a pulp.

Galantine

1 pound round steak
1 pound raw ham
2 eggs
1¾ cups bread crumbs
¼ teaspoon nutmeg
¼ teaspoon pepper
1 teaspoon salt
Juice 1 Sunkist lemon
Grated rind of 1 Sunkist lemon

Put the meat through a food-chopper; add eggs, well beaten, and remaining ingredients; pack into a well-greased breadpan; cover with buttered paper, and steam four hours. Serve cold, thinly sliced.

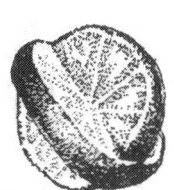  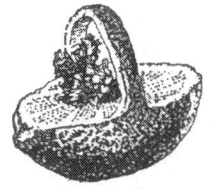

Sunkist Lemon Garnishings

Sunkist Recipes

Sardines with Japanese Rice

Japanese Rice

¼ cup rice
4 cups boiling salted water
2 hard-cooked eggs
2 tablespoons chopped red pepper
2 tablespoons chopped green pepper
1 tablespoon chopped parsley
1 tablespoon scraped onion
1 tablespoon Sunkist lemon juice
½ teaspoon salt
Sardines
Lettuce
French dressing

Wash rice; cook in boiling, salted water five minutes, then steam until soft. Add to rice the finely-chopped eggs, red and green peppers, parsley, scraped onion, Sunkist lemon juice, and salt. Press through a potato-ricer. Arrange on platter, with sardines in the centre and lettuce around the dish, and serve with French dressing.

Sardines, with Lemon

1 box sardines
1 Sunkist lemon
1 bunch radishes
Parsley or watercress

Remove cover neatly and entirely from a box of sardines. Place on a platter, and surround with a wreath of parsley or cress. Cut radishes in the shape of flowers, and arrange in the parsley. Cut lemons in halves, crosswise, and then cut in deep points. Arrange at ends and sides of platter, in the parsley. Serve very cold.

Caviare Canapes

Season Russian Caviaré with a few drops of Sunkist lemon juice. Cut bread in one-fourth-inch slices, then in rounds or rectangles. Toast on one side, and spread untoasted side with seasoned caviaré. Decorate edges with chopped white of hard-cooked egg and cooked yolk, forced through a strainer, and serve on doilies, on individual plates, for a first course.

Sunkist Recipes

German Sour Beef

2 cups water
½ cup Sunkist lemon juice
½ teaspoon salt
⅛ teaspoon pepper
1 large onion
1 carrot
2 pounds cheap cut of beef

Cut onion in thin slices; cut carrot in strips; add water, Sunkist lemon juice, salt and pepper, and pour over the beef, and leave over night. Drain meat; put in small agate pan; dredge meat with flour, and put in hot oven until flour is brown. Add one cup of the water in which meat was soaked, and cover closely. Bake slowly, and, when half done, add vegetables, drained from water, and continue the cooking, adding more liquid, as needed. When tender, remove to serving-dish, and thicken gravy, of which there should be one cup, with two tablespoons flour, mixed with two tablespoons cold liquid. Add, if desired, one-fourth cup sour cream. Put vegetables around the beef, and serve gravy in a sauceboat.

The lemon juice helps very much to make tough meats tender.

Mousselaine Sauce

2 egg yolks
¼ cup cream
½ teaspoon salt
⅛ teaspoon nutmeg
Juice ½ Sunkist lemon
2 tablespoons butter

Mix all the ingredients except the butter in a double boiler, and cook over hot water, stirring constantly until mixture thickens. Add butter, bit by bit, beating it well, and when butter is melted, use at once. Serve with asparagus.

Court Bouillon

2 cups cold water
3 slices carrot
1 slice onion
1 sprig parsley
2 tablespoons Sunkist lemon juice
Bit of bay leaf
¼ teaspoon peppercorns
1 teaspoon salt

Put ingredients in saucepan, adding head and bones of fish, if at hand; bring to boiling point and cook thirty minutes, or until reduced to one cup. Use, for sauces, fish aspic, to flavor the water in which fish is cooked, or as a foundation of a fish soup.

Egg Sauce

1 cup court bouillon
3 tablespoons butter
2 tablespoons flour
1 hard-cooked egg
Salt
Pepper

Melt two tablespoons butter; add flour, and, when smooth, add court bouillon, stirring until it boils. Season to taste, with salt and pepper; add remaining butter and egg thinly sliced or chopped. Or, omit hard-cooked egg, and add two egg yolks, slightly beaten, and Sunkist lemon juice, to taste.

Hollandaise Sauce

½ cup butter
Yolks of 2 eggs
¼ teaspoon salt
Few grains cayenne
1 tablespoon Sunkist lemon juice

Wash butter; divide in three pieces, and put one piece with egg yolks and lemon juice in a saucepan. Work together until smooth, and set saucepan over hot water,

Sunkist Recipes

stirring constantly until butter begins to melt. Then add second piece of butter, and, as it thickens, the third piece, lifting saucepan occasionally from water, that sauce may not curdle. Season with salt and cayenne, and serve immediately. If sauce curdles, add one tablespoon of heavy cream or two tablespoons white sauce, and beat well. For a thinner sauce, add one-third cup boiling water, and cook one minute. Serve with fish, steak, or vegetables.

Horseradish Hollandaise Sauce

To Hollandaise Sauce add three tablespoons grated horseradish root and two tablespoons heavy cream.

Mock Hollandaise Sauce

2 tablespoons butter
2 tablespoons flour—½ cup milk
½ teaspoon salt—⅛ teaspoon pepper
Few grains cayenne
2 egg yolks—½ cup butter
1 tablespoon Sunkist lemon juice

Melt butter; add flour, and stir until well blended; then add milk, salt, pepper, and cayenne, and bring to boiling point. Stir in the egg yolks, butter (bit by bit), and Sunkist lemon juice. Serve immediately.

Orange Marmalade Bavarian Cream

1 tablespoon gelatine
¼ cup cold water
1 cup Sunkist orange marmalade
1 tablespoon Sunkist lemon juice
1 cup heavy cream

Soak gelatine in cold water for five minutes; dissolve by setting the dish of gelatine in one of hot water. When dissolved, add the orange marmalade, in which the peel has been finely chopped; add lemon juice, and fold in the cream, beaten stiff. Mold, chill, and serve with raspberry or strawberry jam, or with fresh strawberries.

For individual service, pin a piece of stiff white paper around paper charlotte russe cups or punch-glasses, making them one inch higher. Put in Bavarian Cream until cup is two-thirds full; add a layer of raspberry jam; then enough Bavarian Cream to come to top of paper. When firm, remove the paper and garnish with a whole strawberry, from the jam, pieces of orange peel, from orange marmalade, and whipped cream, sweetened, flavored, and forced through pastry-bag and tube.

Sunkist Orange Marmalade, with Bavarian Cream

Sunkist Recipes

Orange Marmalade

6 *Sunkist oranges*
1 *Sunkist lemon*
11 *cups cold water*
7 *cups sugar*

Peel oranges, removing all white skin, and slice thin. Slice lemon with rind on; cover oranges and lemon with cold water; let stand twenty-four hours. Then boil three hours; add sugar, and let boil one hour. Pour into glasses; cool, and cover. This recipe makes nine glasses of marmalade.

Orange and Lemon Marmalade

3 *Sunkist oranges*
2 *Sunkist lemons*
5 *cups sugar*
5 *cups water*

Wipe fruit, and cut, crosswise, in as thin slices as possible, removing seeds. Put into preserving kettle, add water, and let stand thirty-six hours. Place on range, bring to boiling point, and let boil (not simmer) two hours. Add sugar, and boil one hour. Turn into sterile glasses, let stand until firm, and cover with melted paraffin.

Orange Jelly

2 *tablespoons gelatine*
½ *cup cold water*
½ *cup boiling water*
½ *cup sugar*
1 *cup Sunkist orange juice*
3 *tablespoons Sunkist lemon juice*

Soak gelatine five minutes in cold water; dissolve in boiling water; add sugar, Sunkist orange and lemon juice, and strain into a mold. Put in a cold place to stiffen. Cut in cubes, and serve in orange baskets, or in half skins of oranges, cut in points. Blood oranges make a very pretty jelly. This jelly may be used as suggested under Lemon Jelly.

Conserve

2 *pounds rhubarb*
3 *cups sugar*
½ *cup seeded raisins*
1 *Sunkist orange*
½ *Sunkist lemon*
1 *cup walnut meats*

Wash rhubarb; cut in one-inch pieces; sprinkle with sugar; add raisins and Sunkist orange and lemon, cut in thin slices, rejecting seeds. Let stand until juice accumulates, then boil, gently, until thick, stirring frequently, to prevent burning. Add nut meats, boil two minutes, and pour into glasses or jars.

One and one-half pounds plums, one quart of cranberries, with one quart cold water, or grapes, from which the seeds are removed, may be used in place of the rhubarb.

Lemon Honey

6 *tablespoons butter*
1 *cup sugar*
3 *egg yolks*
1 *large Sunkist lemon*

Cream butter; add sugar gradually; then heat in double boiler until butter is melted. Add yolks of eggs beaten until thick and lemon-colored, and grated rind of lemon. Stir until it begins to thicken; add juice of the lemon, and continue stirring until the consistency of honey. Turn into two sterilized jelly glasses, and cover.

Sunkist Recipes

Orange Bavarian Cream

½ cup Sunkist orange juice
1 teaspoon grated Sunkist orange rind
½ cup sugar
2 egg yolks
1 tablespoon gelatine
¼ cup cold water
1 cup heavy cream

Heat Sunkist orange juice, rind, and half the sugar in double boiler. Beat egg yolks with remaining sugar; add orange juice mixture, and cook over hot water, stirring until smooth and thickened; add gelatine, dissolved in cold water; then strain into the cream. Set dish containing mixture in a pan of ice-water, and beat until it begins to stiffen. Mold, chill, and serve, garnished with candied orange straws, or with Sunkist orange sections, free from membrane, and sprinkled with sugar.

Lemon Bavarian Cream

½ cup sugar
¼ cup Sunkist lemon juice
2 egg yolks
½ tablespoon gelatine
1 tablespoon cold water
2 egg whites
½ cup cream

Put one-half the sugar and Sunkist lemon juice in double boiler; when heated, pour over egg yolks, beaten with remaining sugar; return to double boiler, and cook, stirring constantly, until thickened. Add gelatine, soaked in cold water; beat occasionally, until cool; fold in egg whites, beaten stiff, and cream, also beaten stiff.

Cumberland Sauce for Duck

Juice 1 Sunkist orange
Juice 1 Sunkist lemon
Grated rind 1 Sunkist lemon
Grated rind 1 Sunkist orange
1 cup powdered sugar
1 tablespoon grated horseradish
2 tablespoons currant jelly

Mix ingredients; beat thoroughly; heat, and serve.

Princess Sauce

3 tablespoons butter
2 tablespoons flour
⅓ teaspoon salt
Few grains pepper
1 cup milk
½ tablespoon Sunkist lemon juice
1 teaspoon beef extract

Melt butter, add flour mixed with salt and pepper; when smooth, add the milk, and stir until it boils. Add Sunkist lemon juice and extract, and one tablespoon butter, bit by bit. Serve with vegetables.

Orange Mint Sauce for Lamb

Remove currant jelly from tumbler to glass serving-dish, and sprinkle with one and one-half tablespoons finely-chopped mint leaves and shavings from rind of one-fourth of a Sunkist orange. Serve with lamb chops or roast lamb.

Orange Vinegar

Put the juice from six Sunkist oranges in a glass jar; add a cake of compressed yeast, dissolved in a little of the juice; cover with cheesecloth, and let stand in a warm place about a month, or until sour enough to use. Strain, and use in place of cider vinegar.

Sunkist Recipes

Sunkist Orange Jelly

Orange Jelly, without Gelatine

Wash six Sunkist oranges and three Sunkist lemons; cut in very thin slices; measure; add three times the measure of water; boil hard for one hour; strain through double cheesecloth, and let stand twenty-four hours. Pour off all the clear liquid; to it, add an equal quantity of sugar; boil until it drips like jelly from a spoon. Put into sterile glasses, and when firm, cover with melted paraffin.

Orange and Rhubarb Sauce

2 pounds rhubarb
2 Sunkist oranges
1½ cups sugar
1 tablespoon granulated gelatine
1 tablespoon cold water

Wash rhubarb, cut into inch pieces; peel oranges, removing membrane with peel, and cut in small pieces; put rhubarb, Sunkist orange and sugar in an earthenware or glass baking-dish, and bake about one hour. Dissolve gelatine in cold water, add to rhubarb mixture, and when cool, fill individual pastry shells with sauce, and decorate with whipped cream, forced through pastry bag and rose tube.

Orange Jelly, with Fruit

Remove sections free from membrane (see page 12) from three Sunkist oranges, and arrange five sections in the bottom of a mold, to form a star. Cover with orange jelly, and when firm, fill mold with orange jelly, mixed with remaining orange, cut in small pieces. Chill, and when firm, remove from mold, and serve with cream. Other fruits or a mixture of fruits and nuts, may be used.

Sunkist Recipes

Banana Canoes

4 bananas
2 Sunkist oranges
2 slices pineapple
Salad dressing
Berries or candied cherries

With a sharp knife cut a section of skin from the concave curve of the bananas, and carefully take out the fruit, leaving the skin in the shape of a canoe. Pare oranges; remove sections, and cut in pieces. mix with pineapple (cut in pieces) and an equal amount of banana pulp (cut in pieces). Fill canoes with fruit; cover with Mayonnaise or French dressing; sprinkle generously with paprika; lay on bed of shredded lettuce, and garnish with berries or candied cherries.

Orange Pinwheels

1 cup flour
2 teaspoons baking-powder
½ teaspoon salt
2 tablespoons butter
⅓ cup milk
2 tablespoons sugar
½ tablespoon Sunkist orange juice
Grated Sunkist orange rind

Mix and sift flour, baking-powder and salt, rub in one tablespoon butter, or other shortening, and moisten to a dough with milk. Roll thin; spread with remaining butter, sprinkle with sugar, mixed with Sunkist orange juice and rind, and roll up like a jelly-roll. Cut in slices, and place, cut side up, in buttered muffin-pans. Sprinkle with remaining sugar, and bake in a hot oven. When small and dainty, these are good for afternoon tea.

Lemon Catsup

Grated rind of 4 Sunkist lemons
Juice of 4 Sunkist lemons
1 tablespoon grated horseradish
1 teaspoon salt
2 teaspoons white mustard seed
2 teaspoons celery seed
4 cloves
Few blades mace
Few grains red pepper

Mix ingredients; boil thirty-five minutes, and bottle while hot. Let stand five or six weeks to ripen. Serve with fish.

Orange Sweet Pickle

4 Sunkist oranges
2 cups sugar
1⅓ cups vinegar
1 teaspoon cloves
1 teaspoon stick cinnamon

Peel Sunkist oranges, removing all white membrane with peel; cut into thick slices; steam until tender and translucent. Boil sugar, vinegar and spices, tied in cheesecloth, for twenty-five minutes. Add fruit, and put in fireless cooker, or simmer slowly, on back of stove, for one hour. Place in glass jar, and let stand a week or two to ripen, before using.

Grapefruit Marmalade

1 Sunkist orange
1 Sunkist lemon
1 grapefruit
Water
Sugar

Slice fruit very thinly, rejecting only seeds and core of the grapefruit. Measure fruit, and add to it three times the quantity of water. Let it stand in an earthen dish over night, and, next morning, boil for ten minutes only. Leave until next day, then boil two hours.

Sunkist Recipes

Measure, add an equal amount of sugar, and boil, stirring occasionally, that it may not burn, about an hour, or until it sheets from spoon. Pour into sterile glasses; let stand covered with cheesecloth, until firm, then cover with melted paraffin.

Lemon Butter

¼ cup butter
¼ teaspoon paprika
1 tablespoon Sunkist lemon juice

Cream the butter and paprika together, and then add Sunkist lemon juice, drop by drop, stirring, constantly, until all the lemon juice is blended with butter.

Maitre d'Hotel Butter

¼ cup butter
½ teaspoon salt
⅛ teaspoon paprika
½ tablespoon finely chopped parsley
¾ tablespoon Sunkist lemon juice

Put butter in a bowl, and work with a wooden spoon until it is soft and creamy; add salt, paprika, chopped parsley, and lemon juice, drop by drop. Serve with steak or chops.

Pepper Butter

¼ cup butter
¼ tablespoon chopped red pepper
¼ tablespoon chopped green pepper
¼ tablespoon chopped parsley
1 teaspoon chopped onion
½ chopped clove of garlic
2 teaspoons Sunkist lemon juice

Cream butter; add other ingredients, and mix well. Serve on broiled steak or chicken.

Candied Sunkist Orange Peel

Put peel from eight Sunkist oranges in cold water; heat to boiling point, and cook gently, until very tender. Drain; put in cold water, and, when cold, remove membrane and soft portion. Boil one cup sugar and one-half cup water until syrup spins a thread; put in peel, and cook gently, until syrup is evaporated and peel looks clear. Drain on wire cake cooler, and leave in open air until thoroughly dry. Store, and use as required in cakes and puddings.

Candied Lemon Peel may be prepared in the same way.

Orange Loaf-Sugar

Cut sugar
Sunkist oranges

Rub the entire surface of blocks of sugar over the rind of Sunkist oranges that have been washed and wiped dry. Store in a glass jar, and use as required; or, roll the blocks of orange sugar, force through a coarse strainer, and use like plain sugar.

Lemon Loaf-Sugar

Cut sugar
Sunkist lemons

Use Sunkist lemons, and follow directions for making orange loaf-sugar.

Sunkist Orange and Lemon Cut Sugar

Sunkist Recipes

For the Preserve Closet

Strawberry Jelly

With a sharp knife remove all the outside, thin, yellow rind from Sunkist oranges. Squeeze out the juice and, with a spoon, scrape off any remaining pulp. Put the thick, white, inner peel through a meat-chopper (there should be one cupful); add the juice of one Sunkist lemon, and let stand one hour. Add three cups water; bring to boiling point, and boil five minutes. Let stand over night. Again bring to boiling point; boil ten minutes, and add one quart strawberries, hulled, washed, drained, and mashed, and boil fifteen minutes, or until juice is extracted from strawberries. Drain through canton flannel jelly bag. Bring juice to boiling point; boil five to seven minutes; measure; add an equal quantity of sugar; boil five minutes, and pour into sterilized jelly glasses.

If a stiffer jelly is desired, use more white skin from Sunkist oranges.

If a larger quantity of jelly is to be made at one time, it will be necessary to proportionately increase the length of time for boiling.

Mint Jelly, with Orange Pectin

Heat two cups of Orange Pectin Extraction to the boiling point; boil five minutes; add two cups sugar and vegetable color paste, to tint a delicate green, and boil five minutes. Add two drops of oil of peppermint; mix well, and turn into sterilized jelly glasses.

Sunkist Recipes

Jellied Oranges, Cut in Sections

Remove a piece one inch in diameter from the navel ends of Sunkist oranges. Remove juice and pulp with a teaspoon, and strain through cheesecloth. With first two fingers take out as much as possible of the white inner membrane from the orange skin. Use juice to make orange jelly, and fill orange skins. Place in upright position in a pan of crushed ice, and leave until firm. Cut in halves, then in thirds, and serve with or without whipped cream.

Pineapple Jelly

1 tablespoon gelatine
¼ cup cold water
½ cup boiling water
½ cup canned pineapple syrup
3 tablespoons Sunkist lemon juice
⅔ cup sugar
3 tablespoons pineapple cubes
3 tablespoons Maraschino cherries
3 tablespoons cut walnut meats
3 tablespoons cubes of orange

Soak gelatine in cold water; dissolve in boiling water, and add pineapple syrup, Sunkist lemon juice, and sugar. When gelatine is beginning to get stiff, stir in the fruit and nuts, of which there should be, in all, three-fourths of a cup. Turn into a mold, and chill.

Lemon Jelly

1½ cups cold water
1 cup sugar
4 cloves
½-inch stick cinnamon
1 tablespoon gelatine
2 tablespoons cold water
¼ cup Sunkist lemon juice
Few grains salt

Put sugar, water, cloves and cinnamon in saucepan; place on range; stir until sugar has dissolved, and bring to boiling point. Add gelatine which has soaked in cold water five minutes. Stir until gelatine has dissolved; then add Sunkist lemon juice and salt. Strain into a mold, dipped into cold water, and chill. Spices may be omitted.

For Macedoine Pudding, add, when jelly begins to stiffen, a mixture of fruits, cut in pieces and drained. Mold and chill.

For Lemon Sponge, when mixture begins to stiffen, beat with egg-beater until very light and frothy. Mold and chill.

For Jelly in Layers, divide jelly in three portions, and put one portion in bottom of mold. When firm, decorate, if desired, with candied cherries, and cover with a second portion, beaten until light. When that is firm, cover with a layer of plain jelly. Mold, chill, cut in slices, and serve. The different layers may be colored pink and green.

For Snow Pudding, add to lemon sponge the stiffly-beaten whites of two eggs. Mold, chill, and serve with boiled custard.

Mint Jelly, with Gelatine

5 sprigs mint
⅔ cup water
1¼ tablespoons gelatine
½ cup cold water
½ cup sugar
Juice of 1 Sunkist lemon
Green color paste

Boil sprigs of mint and two-thirds cup of water for five minutes. Soak gelatine in one-half cup cold water; add to boiling mint and water, with sugar and Sunkist lemon juice. Color a delicate green with vegetable color paste; strain into four small molds; chill, and serve with roast lamb or lamb chops.

Sunkist Recipes

Lemon Pectin Extraction

Use the inner white peel of Sunkist lemons, and follow directions for Orange Pectin Extraction.

Orange Pectin Extraction

With a sharp knife remove every particle of the outside, thin, yellow rind from Sunkist oranges. Remove the white peel from the orange and put it through a meat chopper. To each cupful, pressed down, of chopped white peel, add the juice of one Sunkist lemon, and let stand one hour. Add two cups of water; heat to boiling point, and let boil five minutes. Let stand over night; add four cups of water; heat to boiling point, and boil ten minutes. Strain through a canton flannel jelly bag. This extraction can be poured at once into sterile bottles and kept until needed, or flavored, as desired, and made into jelly.

Lemon Extract

When only the juice is to be used from a number of Sunkist lemons, carefully wash and wipe the the fruit; then grate the yellow rind off, being particular that not any white inner skin is grated. Put yellow grated rind into a small bottle, cover with pure grain alcohol, cork tightly, and set away for several weeks. Strain, and the extract is ready for use.

Sunkist orange extract is made in the same way.

Orange Fritters

2 Sunkist oranges
1 egg
¼ cup milk
½ cup flour
⅓ teaspoon baking-powder
½ teaspoon sugar
¼ teaspoon salt
½ tablespoon cooking oil

Beat egg until light; add milk, flour, sifted with baking-powder, sugar and salt, and oil or melted butter. Beat until smooth. Pare Sunkist oranges, removing membrane with peel; cut in slices, and sprinkle with sugar and a few drops Sunkist lemon juice. Have deep fat, hot enough to brown a piece of bread while counting to sixty. Dip orange sections in batter mixture, and fry in deep fat until puffed and brown. Do not fry too many at one time. Drain on brown paper; sprinkle with powdered sugar, and serve with orange sauce.

Sweet Croquettes

1 cup stale cake crumbs
¼ cup chopped, blanched almonds or shredded cocoanut
Grated rind ½ Sunkist lemon
½ tablespoon Sunkist lemon juice
½ cup Sunkist orange juice
1 egg yolk
1 egg white
Fine cake crumbs

Mix first four ingredients in saucepan; add Sunkist orange juice, to moisten, and let stand ten minutes. Heat to boiling point; remove from fire; add egg yolk, and cool. Shape as croquettes; dip in egg white, beaten slightly, with one tablespoon cold water; roll in sifted dry bread or cake crumbs, and fry in deep fat. Sprinkle with powdered sugar, and serve with chocolate sauce.

Sunkist Recipes

Orange Fondant

2 cups sugar
½ cup Sunkist orange juice
Yellow rind 1 Sunkist orange

Put sugar, Sunkist orange juice and a few pieces of yellow orange rind in saucepan, and boil to 238 degrees, or until syrup spins a long thread.

Pour onto a marble slab or a large white agate tray or platter, and leave until cool. Remove orange rind, and work syrup with a broad spatula, or a wooden butter-hand, until it gets white and creamy; then knead until smooth. Keep covered in a glass jar until wanted, coloring with yellow color paste, if a deeper color is desired.

Orange Bonbons. For the centres, shape fondant in small balls, and leave on paraffin paper several hours or over night. Place more fondant in small saucepan, over hot water, and stir until melted. Drop centres, one at a time, in the melted fondant, removing with candy-dipper, or a two-tined fork, to paraffin paper. Nuts, candied cherries or orange straws may be dipped in the fondant. Fondant balls may be dipped in melted chocolate.

Orange Cocoanut Creams. Melt one cup orange fondant over hot water; stir in one cup shredded cocoanut, using, if possible, the long shreds for sale by wholesale confectioners. Drop from two-tined fork, in irregular mounds, on paraffin paper.

Orange Mints. Melt orange fondant over hot water; then drop from tip of spoon, in perfect rounds, on paraffin paper.

Rhubarb Jelly

Follow directions for making strawberry jelly, using rhubarb in place of strawberries.

Orange Straws

Follow directions for candied orange peel, cutting peel in thin strips with scissors after the first cooking. When dry, roll in granulated sugar, and store in glass jars.

Chocolate Candied Orange Peel

Candied orange peel
Confectioners' chocolate

Melt confectioners' dipping chocolate in saucepan over hot water. Let water come to the boiling point; then remove from fire, and chocolate will melt. It should not be allowed to reach a higher temperature than 125 degrees. Beat until cool (about 82 degrees); then dip each piece of candied orange peel, separately, in the chocolate; put on paraffin paper, or piece of white oilcloth, and cool quickly.

Sunkist Orange Bonbons

Sunkist Recipes

Spinach, with Sunkist Lemon and Hollandaise Sauce

Spinach, with Sunkist Lemon

Wash one peck Spinach thoroughly, and steam over hot water until tender. Chop fine; season with salt and paprika. Of three hard-cooked eggs, reserve some for garnish, and put remainder through potato-ricer. Add to spinach, and reheat with three tablespoons butter; add two tablespoons Sunkist lemon juice; garnish with roses, cut from hard-cooked white of egg, and serve with Horseradish Hollandaise Sauce. Serve with lamb chops or cutlets.

Arlington Asparagus

Cut rings one-third inch wide from a lemon, and remove the pulp. Cut crusts from oblong pieces of toast, and moisten with water, in which asparagus has been cooked. Put stalks of boiled asparagus through lemon peel rings, and arrange on toast. Brush rings with melted butter, and serve very hot, with Hollandaise Sauce, Mousselaine Sauce, or melted butter, poured over the asparagus.

Oyster Plant, with Fine Herbs

1 bunch oyster plant
Juice 1 Sunkist lemon
3 tablespoons butter
1 teaspoon chopped parsley
½ teaspoon chopped chives
Salt
Pepper

Wash and scrape oyster plant. Put at once into cold water with the lemon juice, and let stand ten minutes. Cut, crosswise, in one-inch slices, and cook in boiling salted water, to cover, until soft; drain; add three tablespoons butter, and reheat. Sprinkle with parsley, chives, salt and pepper, and serve.

Artichokes, Italian Style

2 French artichokes
1 Sunkist lemon
Parsley
1 teaspoon sweet herbs
¾ cup brown stock
½ cup tomatoes
½ cup mushroom liquor

Cut artichokes in quarters, and remove the choke. Rub over with Sunkist lemon; parboil fifteen minutes in water with one-half tea-

Sunkist Recipes

spoon salt and one tablespoon Sunkist lemon juice, and drain. Place in casserole, with sweet herbs, brown stock and two teaspoons Sunkist lemon juice. Cover, and cook in oven until tender. Remove; strain liquor in pan; add to it tomatoes, stewed and strained, mushroom liquor, and one-half tablespoon chopped parsley. Cook ten minutes; season, to taste, and pour over artichokes.

Beet Relish

1 cup cooked beets
3 tablespoons horseradish
2 teaspoons powdered sugar
1 teaspoon salt
4 tablespoons lemon juice

Chop the beets, which should be cold, and add other ingredients. Serve with cold sliced meat.

Carrots and Turnips, Princess

1 cup carrot strips
1 cup turnip cubes
1 cup Princess Sauce
Chopped parsley

Wash and scrape carrots, and cut in two-inch strips. Wash and pare white turnips, and cut in half-inch cubes. Steam until tender; moisten with Princess Sauce (see page 20), and sprinkle with chopped parsley.

Cauliflower Mousselaine

Remove leaves; cut off stalk, and soak cauliflower thirty minutes, head down, in cold water, to cover. Cook, head up, twenty minutes, or until soft, in boiling water, to which is added one tablespoon, each, of salt and lemon juice. Drain; separate into flowerets, and over it pour Mousselaine Sauce.

Princess Potatoes

Wash and pare large potatoes, and shape with an apple-corer; then cut the cylinders thus made into half-inch lengths, crosswise. Soak in cold water; drain; cook in boiling salted water two minutes; then let stand ten minutes in ice-water. Drain; dry with towels, and fry in deep fat until soft, but not brown. When all potato is fried, put it back into frying-basket, and plunge it altogether in very hot fat, and fry until crisp and brown. Drain on brown paper; put in serving-dish, and cover with Princess Sauce.

Sauted Tomatoes

Wipe, and remove slices from top and bottom of tomatoes. Cut in halves, crosswise, sprinkle with salt, pepper, and flour, and saute in butter. Remove to circular pieces of sauted bread, and on each put a tablespoon of Horseradish Hollandaise Sauce.

Sunkist Orange Basket

Sunkist Orange Basket

Sunkist Recipes

Lemon Honey Sandwiches

1 cream cheese
4 tablespoons lemon honey
Bread

Work the cheese with a silver fork until it is soft; add lemon honey, and mix. Cut bread in thin slices; spread with mixture; put together in pairs, and cut in triangles or strips. This mixture can be spread on thin crackers, and sprinkled with chopped nuts.

Orange Honey Sandwiches

1 cup sugar
¼ cup water
¼ cup Sunkist orange juice
½ cup finely-chopped Sunkist orange peel
½ teaspoon vanilla

Boil sugar, water and orange juice until syrup will spin a thread when dropped from tip of spoon. Add orange peel, from which the white must be removed before peel is chopped, and one-half teaspoon vanilla. Again bring to boiling point; cool, and use as sandwich filling between thin slices of buttered bread.

Savory Butter Sandwiches

2 teaspoons Sunkist lemon juice
2 teaspoons anchovy paste
2 teaspoons mustard
4 teaspoons Roquefort cheese
4 tablespoons butter

Put all ingredients into a bowl; beat until smooth and creamy; spread on crackers; cover each with another cracker, and use with cocktails or simple salads.

Orange Bread

1 yeast cake
¼ cup lukewarm water
1 egg
1 tablespoon melted butter
1 tablespoon melted lard
1 teaspoon salt
2 tablespoons sugar
Grated rind 2 Sunkist oranges
¾ cup Sunkist orange juice
3 cups flour

Dissolve yeast in warm water; add egg well beaten, butter, lard, salt, sugar, grated Sunkist orange rind, Sunkist orange juice, and flour. Beat until smooth, adding more flour, if necessary; knead until smooth and elastic; let rise till double its bulk; shape in double loaf; put in breadpan; let rise again to double its bulk, and bake one hour in a moderate oven. This bread is delicious with orange marmalade for afternoon tea.

Orange Peel Bread

1 cup scalded milk
3 tablespoons molasses
1 teaspoon salt
1 yeast cake
⅓ cup lukewarm water
1½ cups bread flour
1½ cups Graham flour
½ cup candied orange peel
½ cup pecan nut meats

Mix milk, molasses and salt; when lukewarm, add yeast cake, dissolved in lukewarm water, and flour; mix; then add orange peel (see page 23) and nuts, cut in small pieces. When thoroughly mixed, let rise until double its bulk; cut down with

Sunkist Recipes

caseknife, and fill small buttered baking-powder boxes one-third full; let rise to double its bulk, and bake in a moderate oven. This mixture can be baked in muffin-tins, and served while hot.

Colonial Sandwiches

Slice cold orange peel bread (see page 30) as thinly as possible; spread with creamed butter, and serve on a fancy plate, covered with a doily.

Toasted Marmalade Sandwiches

Cut two thin slices of bread, spread with butter; then spread lightly with Sunkist orange marmalade. Put slices together, toast, cut in halves crosswise, and serve immediately.

Sliced Sunkist Lemon, Nut Cloves and Cherries

Sunkist Recipes

Salads and Dressings
Desserts and Beverages

Orange and Peanut Salad
1 banana
2 Sunkist oranges
½ cup peanuts
Lettuce
French dressing

Remove skin from banana; scrape, and cut in quarters (lengthwise) and thirds (crosswise), and roll in peanuts, finely chopped. Pare oranges, cut in slices (crosswise); stamp out centre, and insert a piece of banana through each slice. Arrange on bed of lettuce, and serve with French dressing.

Peanut Rice Salad
3 tablespoons rice
Boiling salted water
1 cup Sunkist orange juice
½ cup finely-chopped peanuts
Cream cheese balls
Lettuce
French dressing

Wash rice; cook seven minutes in boiling salted water. Drain; cover with orange juice, and cook, in double boiler, until rice is tender. Cool; mix (using a fork) with finely-chopped peanuts; sprinkle with salt; arrange on lettuce leaves with small balls made from cream cheese, and serve with French dressing.

New York Salad
4 slices pineapple
½ cup celery
½ cup nuts chopped
2 Sunkist oranges
Cream mayonnaise
Lettuce

Arrange slices of pineapple on nests of lettuce leaves. Cut celery

Sunkist Recipes

in slender strips, one and one-half inches long, and mix with nut meats. Pile in centre of pineapple, and garnish with four sections of Sunkist orange, free from membrane, laid symmetrically on pineapple. Pass dressing separately.

Fig and Cheese Salad

Mix cream cheese with pignolia nuts that have been browned in the oven. Season with salt and moisten with Sunkist orange juice or cream. Fill fresh or canned figs with cheese mixture; arrange on lettuce leaves; garnish with thin slices of Sunkist oranges, cut in quarters and sprinkled with finely-chopped pignolia nuts, and serve with Honey Dressing (see page 34).

Mock Lobster Salad

2 cups cooked haddock
2 cups celery
2 tablespoons pimento
1 cup mayonnaise dressing
2 tablespoons Sunkist lemon juice

Mix cold, flaked, boiled haddock with finely-chopped pimento; season with salt, paprika, and Sunkist lemon juice, and let stand one-half hour. Add celery, finely chopped, and two tablespoons mayonnaise dressing. Stir lightly; pile on crisp lettuce leaves, and cover with dressing. Garnish with Sunkist lemon, cut in fancy shapes and decorated with paprika.

Ginger Ale Fruit Salad

1½ tablespoons gelatine
2 tablespoons cold water
⅓ cup boiling water
1 cup ginger ale
2 tablespoons sugar
Few grains salt
Juice 1 Sunkist lemon
½ cup white grapes
½ cup apple dice
½ cup celery
½ cup canned pineapple cubes
¼ cup preserved ginger
Cream mayonnaise dressing

Soak gelatine in cold water; dissolve in boiling water; add ginger ale, sugar, salt, and Sunkist lemon juice. When jelly begins to set, fold in white grapes (skinned and seeded), apples (pared, cored, and cut in small pieces), celery (cut in small strips), pineapple (shredded), and ginger (cut fine). Turn into a ring mold; chill, and serve on lettuce leaves. Fill centre with Cream Mayonnaise Dressing (see page 35).

Jellied Vegetable Salad

1 tablespoon gelatine
¼ cup cold water
1 cup boiling water
¼ cup sugar
6 tablespoons Sunkist lemon juice
1 teaspoon salt
½ cup celery, cut in pieces
½ cup cooked peas
½ cup shredded cabbage
1½ canned pimentoes

Soak gelatine in cold water, and dissolve in boiling water; then add sugar, Sunkist lemon juice, and salt. Strain; cool, and when beginning to stiffen, add celery (cut in small pieces), cabbage (finely shredded), peas, and pimento (cut in small pieces). Turn into a mold, and put in a cold place to stiffen. Unmold, and serve on lettuce, with Cream French Dressing (see page 35).

French Dressing

½ teaspoon salt
¼ teaspoon paprika
4 tablespoons oil
2 tablespoons Sunkist lemon juice

Mix ingredients in order given, and stir or shake thoroughly just before serving. A half-pint glass jar, with screw top, or a French Dressing bottle, are best for mixing.

Sunkist Recipes

Frozen Fruit Salad

1 tablespoon melted butter
2 egg yolks
3½ tablespoons flour
3 tablespoons sugar
1 teaspoon salt
⅓ teaspoon paprika
Few grains cayenne
⅔ cup milk
⅓ cup Sunkist lemon juice
Sunkist orange ⎫
Cherries ⎬ 1 cup in all
Pineapple ⎪
Banana ⎭
1 cup cream

Put butter in double boiler; add well-beaten egg yolks and flour, mixed with sugar, salt, paprika, and cayenne. Then add milk and Sunkist lemon juice; cook, stirring constantly, until mixture thickens. Strain into bowl; beat two minutes; then cool. Add one cup mixed fruit, cut in small pieces; fold in stiffly-beaten cream; put into a pint brick mold or baking-powder boxes; cover with buttered paper and tin cover; pack in ice and salt, and let stand two hours. Cut in slices, and serve on lettuce.

Orange Salad

2 Sunkist oranges
Few grains mustard
French dressing
Watercress

Sunkist Orange Salad

Pare oranges, cut in very thin slices, and slices in quarters. Marinate with French Dressing, to which is added a few grains of mustard, and serve on a bed of watercress.

Honey Salad Dressing

½ cup strained honey
3 egg yolks
½ teaspoon salt
¼ teaspoon paprika
1 tablespoon Sunkist lemon juice
1 cup heavy cream

Heat the strained honey to the boiling point; then pour slowly, while beating constantly, onto well-beaten egg yolks. Cook one minute, stirring constantly; remove from fire, and stir occasionally, until cool. Add salt, paprika and Sunkist lemon juice; and just before using, add cream, beaten until stiff.

Golden Salad Dressing

¼ cup pineapple juice
¼ cup Sunkist orange juice
2 tablespoons Sunkist lemon juice
⅛ teaspoon salt
2 egg yolks
⅓ cup sugar
2 egg whites

Mix pineapple juice, Sunkist orange and lemon juice, and salt, and heat in a double boiler. Beat egg yolks until thick and lemon-colored, gradually adding one-half the sugar; then, while beating constantly, add hot fruit juices; return to double boiler, and cook, stirring constantly until thick and smooth. Beat whites of eggs until stiff; add remaining sugar, and combine with first mixture just before removing from fire.

Sunkist Recipes

Sunkist Star Salad

Star Salad

On individual plates of lettuce arrange, in star pattern, five sections of grapefruit, free from membrane; on these place five sections of Sunkist orange, free from membrane. Cut long, slender strips of figs, and place on edge of Sunkist orange sections. Fill spaces between orange star points with finely-cut dates. Serve with French Dressing, made with Orange Vinegar.

Mayonnaise Dressing

½ teaspoon mustard
½ teaspoon salt
½ teaspoon powdered sugar
Few grains cayenne
1 egg yolk
2 tablespoons Sunkist lemon juice
¾ cup olive or peanut oil

Sift, together, mustard, salt, sugar and cayenne; add egg yolk and one-half teaspoon Sunkist lemon juice. While stirring constantly, add, drop by drop, three teaspoons of oil; then add oil, in a fine, steady stream, continuing the beating, and thinning occasionally with lemon juice, until all the oil and lemon juice is used.

Boiled Salad Dressing

½ tablespoon salt
1 teaspoon mustard
1½ tablespoons sugar
Few grains cayenne
1 tablespoon flour
2 egg yolks
1½ tablespoons butter or oil
¾ cup milk (sweet or sour)
¼ cup Sunkist lemon juice

Mix and sift dry ingredients; add egg yolks, slightly beaten, and milk. Cook over boiling water, stirring until thick. Add butter and Sunkist lemon juice; strain, and cool.

Cream French Dressing

To French Dressing add three tablespoons heavy cream, and shake until well blended.

Martinique French Dressing

To French Dressing add one-half teaspoon finely-chopped parsley and one-half tablespoon finely-chopped green pepper.

Sunkist Recipes

French Dressing, with Orange Vinegar

½ teaspoon salt
¼ teaspoon paprika
4 tablespoons olive oil
2 tablespoons Sunkist orange vinegar

Mix ingredients, in order given, and stir or shake thoroughly in a glass jar just before using.

Marshmallow Salad

2 Sunkist oranges
8 marshmallows
1 slice canned pineapple
Chopped parsley
½ cup white grapes
¼ cup nut meats
Pimento
Golden Fruit Salad Dressing
Lettuce

Cut oranges in two; remove pulp carefully; then pull out all membrane, leaving orange cups. Cut pineapple, marshmallows and nuts in small pieces; skin and seed the grapes before measuring, and mix all with orange pulp and a little dressing. Fill orange cups; cover with dressing, and cross two strips of pimento on the dressing. Place one-half a grape on centre of salad and a bit of chopped parsley between the strips of pimento.

Sunkist Marshmallow Salad

Cream Mayonnaise Dressing

To Mayonnaise Dressing add, just before serving, one-fourth cup heavy cream, beaten stiff.

Russian Salad Dressing

3 tablespoons mayonnaise dressing
2 tablespoons olive oil
1 tablespoon Sunkist lemon juice
1 tablespoon tomato catsup
1 teaspoon chopped green pepper
2 drops Tabasco sauce

Add ingredients, very slowly, to mayonnaise dressing, stirring constantly.

Thousand Island Salad Dressing

½ cup olive oil
Juice ½ Sunkist lemon
Juice ½ Sunkist orange
1 teaspoon grated onion
1 tablespoon chopped parsley
8 sliced olives
8 cooked chestnuts
¼ teaspoon salt
¼ teaspoon paprika
1 teaspoon Worcestershire sauce
¼ teaspoon mustard

Remove shells from chestnuts, and cook in boiling salted water until soft; then cool, and cut in thin slices. Put all the ingredients in a pint glass jar; cover, and shake until smooth and slightly thickened. Serve on Southern lettuce, cut in quarters, carefully washed and drained.

Sunkist Recipes

Orange Fruit Cake

¼ cup butter
⅓ cup sugar
1 egg
⅔ cup Sunkist orange marmalade
2 cups flour
1 teaspoon baking-powder
⅛ teaspoon soda
⅛ teaspoon cinnamon
⅛ teaspoon cloves
⅓ cup chopped raisins
⅓ cup chopped nut meats

Cream the butter; add, gradually, one-half the sugar; beat egg until light; add remaining sugar, and combine mixtures; then add the marmalade. Sift together the flour, soda, baking-powder, cinnamon and cloves, and add to mixture with raisins and nuts. Bake in one loaf in a moderate oven.

Orange Roly-Poly

2 cups flour
4 teaspoons baking-powder
1 teaspoon salt
4 tablespoons butter
¾ cup milk, scant
½ cup sugar
4 Sunkist oranges
Grated rind 1 Sunkist orange
½ cup water

Mix and sift flour, baking-powder, and salt. With tips of fingers rub in two tablespoons butter, and mix, to a dough, with milk. Roll out one-half inch thick, and cover with small pieces of Sunkist orange pulp. Mix sugar, orange rind, and remaining butter, and sprinkle two-thirds of it over the orange. Roll up; pinch ends together; place in baking-dish; sprinkle with remaining sugar, surround with water, and bake about thirty minutes. Serve with an orange or lemon sauce.

Orange Jelly Roll

3 egg whites
3 egg yolks
1 cup sugar
Grated rind 1 Sunkist orange
¼ cup Sunkist orange juice
1 cup flour
1 teaspoon baking-powder
¼ teaspoon salt

Beat egg whites until stiff; add yolks, one at a time, and continue beating; add sugar, gradually; add grated Sunkist orange rind and Sunkist orange juice. Fold in flour, mixed and sifted with baking-powder and salt. Line bottom of dripping-pan with paper, and butter paper and sides of pan. Pour in cake mixture, spread evenly, and bake in a moderate oven twelve minutes. Take from oven and turn onto a paper sprinkled with powdered sugar. Remove paper and cut crusty edges from four sides of cake, working rapidly. Spread with Orange Jelly (see page 19). Roll, and wrap in the sugared paper, that cake may be held in shape.

Orange Pie Filling

1 cup sugar
⅓ cup flour
¼ teaspoon salt
Grated rind 1 Sunkist orange
1 cup Sunkist orange juice
Juice ½ Sunkist lemon
2 tablespoons butter
3 egg yolks

Mix sugar, flour, salt and grated rind; add fruit juice, and cook in double boiler ten minutes, stirring until thickened, and afterward, occasionally. Add butter and egg yolks beaten light; cook two minutes, and cool. Finish like lemon pie.

Sunkist Recipes

Genoa Cake

1 cup butter
Chopped rind 1 Sunkist lemon
1 cup sugar
4 egg yolks
1½ cups flour
¼ teaspoon cinnamon
1 teaspoon baking-powder
¼ teaspoon salt
¼ cup almonds
¼ cup candied cherries
4 egg whites

Cream butter; add yellow rind of Sunkist lemon, finely chopped, and add sugar, gradually. Beat egg yolks until thick and lemon-colored; add to first mixture, and beat thoroughly. Then add flour, sifted with baking-powder, salt, and cinnamon; almonds, blanched and shredded; cherries, cut in small pieces, and egg whites, beaten stiff. Mix well and bake in pan, lined with paper, buttered, and sprinkled with two tablespoons, each, of flour and sugar, sifted together. Shredded cocoanut or raisins may be substituted for the almonds and cherries.

Rolled Orange Wafers

½ cup butter
1 cup sugar
Grated rind 1 Sunkist orange
1 teaspoon soda
1 tablespoon cold water
¼ cup Sunkist orange juice
2 cups flour

Cream butter; gradually add sugar and Sunkist orange rind, beating until light; dissolve soda in cold water; add to Sunkist orange juice, then add, alternately with flour, to first mixture. Spread mixture on well-buttered sheet in the thinnest possible layer, and bake in a moderate oven. When baked, cut in squares; quickly roll each square, while hot, over handle of a wooden spoon, and arrange on a doily-covered plate.

Orange Sponge Cake

2 egg yolks
4 tablespoons Sunkist orange juice
½ tablespoon Sunkist lemon juice
¾ cup sugar
¼ teaspoon grated Sunkist orange rind
2 egg whites
1 cup flour
¼ teaspoon soda

Beat egg yolks with Sunkist orange and lemon juice until thick and yellow; mix sugar and grated Sunkist orange rind, and add, gradually, to egg yolks; add stiffly-beaten egg whites, and cut and fold in flour, sifted four times with soda. Pour into a buttered and floured cakepan, and bake in a moderate oven about forty minutes.

Devil's Food

¼ cup butter
1 cup sugar
2 egg yolks
½ cup milk
1¼ cups flour
3 teaspoons baking-powder
2 egg whites
2 squares chocolate
Grated rind ½ Sunkist orange

Cream butter; add, gradually, one-half the sugar and melted chocolate. Beat yolks of eggs until thick and lemon-colored, and add gradually, the remaining sugar. Combine mixtures, and add milk, alternately, with flour, sifted with baking-powder; then add whites of eggs, beaten stiff, and grated Sunkist orange rind. Bake forty-five to fifty minutes. Frost with Boiled Orange Frosting. When frosting is cool, spread a thin layer of melted chocolate over the top.

Lemon Drop Cookies

⅓ cup butter
½ cup sugar
1 egg
¼ teaspoon soda
2 tablespoons hot water
½ tablespoon Sunkist lemon juice
Grated rind 1 Sunkist lemon
¾ cup flour

Cream butter; add sugar, gradually, and egg, beaten until thick and light, soda, dissolved in hot water, Sunkist lemon juice, grated Sunkist lemon rind, and flour. Mix well, drop from tip of teaspoon onto buttered baking sheet, and bake in a quick oven.

To make crisp cookies, use one and one-half cups flour when mixing; chill thoroughly, roll very thin, sprinkle lightly with sugar, cut out, and bake.

Filled Cookies

½ cup butter
1 cup sugar
1 egg
½ cup milk
2½ cups flour
2 teaspoons baking-powder

Cream the butter, add sugar gradually, and egg well beaten. Mix and sift flour and baking-powder, and add, alternately with milk, to first mixture. Chill, roll out, put a tablespoon of filling in the centre of one cookie, place another on top, and press edges together. Bake on buttered tin sheet in a quick oven. For the filling put one-half cup, each, of chopped raisins, walnuts and sugar in saucepan, add two tablespoons of flour and one-fourth cup boiling water. Bring to the boiling point; add one and one-half tablespoons Sunkist lemon juice; cool, and use as directed.

Lemon Queen Cake

⅓ cup butter
1 cup flour
¼ teaspoon soda
3 egg whites
⅝ cup powdered sugar
¾ tablespoon Sunkist lemon juice

Cream the butter; add, gradually, two-thirds of the flour, sifted with soda; then add Sunkist lemon juice. Beat whites of eggs until stiff; add sugar, gradually, while beating constantly; combine mixtures; then fold in remaining flour. Bake forty minutes in a moderate oven.

Pastry

1¼ cups flour
4 tablespoons lard
½ teaspoon salt
⅓ cup cold water
3 tablespoons butter

Mix flour and salt, and gently rub in lard with tips of fingers. Add cold water, to make a dough; turn on floured cloth, and knead two minutes. Pat with rolling-pin; lift to prevent sticking, and roll out to a long, rectangular piece. Spread two-thirds of it with the butter, which has been washed in cold water to free it from buttermilk; fold over in three layers; turn it one-quarter of the way around; pat, lift, roll, fold, and turn (do this three times). Roll, to fit pie-plate, and bake. This is a particularly good paste for turnovers and tartlet shells.

Sunkist Recipes

Sunkist Orange Cake

Orange Cake

⅓ cup butter
1 cup sugar
2 eggs
½ cup Sunkist orange juice
Grated rind 1 Sunkist orange
1 tablespoon Sunkist lemon juice
1¾ cups flour
½ teaspoon soda

Cream butter; add sugar, gradually, and eggs, beaten until thick and lemon-colored. Sift flour and soda together four times; add alternately with combined fruit juices and rind to first mixture. Put in buttered and floured cake-pan, and bake in a moderate oven thirty-five or forty minutes. Cover with Boiled Orange Frosting (see page 51).

Orange Cake Filling

Grated rind 1 Sunkist orange
½ cup sugar
2 tablespoons cornstarch
⅔ cup boiling water
2 tablespoons butter
1 egg
⅓ cup Sunkist orange juice
1 teaspoon Sunkist lemon juice

Put grated Sunkist orange rind, sugar and cornstarch in saucepan, mix well, pour on boiling water, and cook ten minutes, stirring constantly; then add butter. Pour mixture over well-beaten egg; return to saucepan; stir constantly, and cook one minute. Add Sunkist orange juice and Sunkist lemon juice; beat well, and when cool, use as a filling in layer cake.

Citrus Souffle

1 tablespoon butter
⅛ cup sugar
Juice 2 Sunkist lemons
4 egg yolks
4 eggs whites
2 tablespoons chopped nuts
Grated rind 1 Sunkist lemon

Cream butter; add sugar, gradually, and yolks of eggs, beaten until thick and lemon-colored, strained Sunkist lemon juice and grated Sunkist lemon rind, and beat. Fold in the stiffly-beaten whites of eggs and nuts. Pour into a well-buttered pudding-dish, set in a pan of hot water, and bake from thirty to forty minutes in a moderate oven. Serve immediately.

Sunkist Recipes

Turkish Delight

2 ounces sheet gelatine
1½ cups cold water
1 cup sugar
Grated rind 1 Sunkist orange
Grated rind 1 Sunkist lemon
Juice 1 Sunkist orange
Juice 1 Sunkist lemon
1 cup nut meats

Soak gelatine in one-half cup cold water two hours. Dissolve sugar in remaining water, bring to boiling point; add soaked gelatine, and boil twenty minutes, stirring until gelatine dissolves, and occasionally afterwards. Add juice and rind of Sunkist orange and lemon; strain; add chopped nut meats; pour into buttered pan, and when cool, cut in squares. Roll each piece in confectioners' sugar.

If the knife sticks when cutting the paste, dip the knife into hot water.

Orange Fudge

1½ cups sugar
½ cup milk
2 tablespoons butter
1 tablespoon orange juice
Grated rind ½ orange
¼ cup candied orange peel

Place sugar and milk in saucepan, boil five minutes; add butter, Sunkist orange juice and rind, and boil until stiff enough to form a soft ball when tried in cold water. Remove from fire; cool; beat until creamy; add candied orange peel, cut in small pieces; pour into a buttered pan, and when almost firm mark in squares.

Orange Balls

Soak Sunkist orange peels three days in cold water, changing the water daily; then put in hot water, and boil until soft. Drain, wipe dry with cheesecloth, chop fine, and measure. Take an equal amount of sugar, and for each one-third of a cup of sugar add two tablespoons each of water and butter, and boil until it will spin a thread; then add the chopped peel; boil about five minutes; cool; put on a board, sprinkle with granulated sugar, and shape into small balls. These may be rolled in coarse sugar, and allowed to dry, or they may be dipped in fondant, flavored with vanilla. They are delicious dipped in chocolate, with a few grains of orange sugar sprinkled on the top of each chocolate before it hardens.

Orange Filling

2 Sunkist oranges
2 large apples
1 cup sugar

Grate the rind and squeeze the juice of the Sunkist oranges, add apples pared and grated, and the sugar. Stir and boil fifteen minutes. Cool and use between layers of pastry or cake.

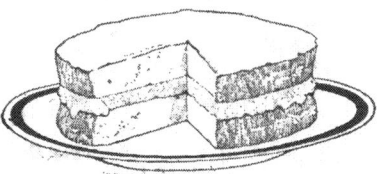

Orange Filling

Sunkist Recipes

Sunkist Lemon Pie

Lemon Pie

1¼ cups sugar
⅓ cup flour
Few grains salt
Juice 1 Sunkist lemon
Grated rind
3 egg yolks
1 cup boiling water
1 teaspoon butter

Mix sugar, flour and salt, add boiling water, stirring constantly. Cook fifteen minutes, then add butter, egg yolks, rind and juice of one lemon. Turn into a pie plate, or preferably a pan that is perforated or made of wire and lined with flaky pastry which has been baked until a golden brown. Make a meringue of three egg whites and add one-half cup of powdered sugar, with a teaspoonful of lemon juice; cover pie with meringue and bake in a moderate oven until brown. Allow to cool before serving.

Fifteen-Dollar Pie

½ cup sugar
2 tablespoons flour
1½ tablespoons melted butter
Juice 1 Sunkist lemon
1 egg yolk
½ cup milk
1 egg white
Few grains salt

Mix sugar and flour, add melted butter, Sunkist lemon juice, egg yolk slightly beaten, milk, egg white stiffly beaten, and salt. Bake in one crust, and cover with meringue or not, as desired.

Lemon Pie with Bread Crumbs

1½ cups soft bread crumbs
3 tablespoons butter
1 cup boiling water
1 cup sugar
1½ teaspoons cornstarch
2 egg yolks
3 tablespoons Sunkist lemon juice
Grated rind 1 Sunkist lemon

Sunkist Recipes

Break bread crumbs in small pieces; add butter, pour boiling water over, and let them stand until soft. Mix sugar and cornstarch, add egg yolks, well beaten, and Sunkist lemon juice and rind. Combine mixtures; bake in one crust, and cover with meringue.

Ada's Lemon Pie

Grated rind 1 Sunkist lemon
2 tablespoons Sunkist lemon juice
1 cup sugar
1 egg yolk
1 tablespoon melted butter
2 tablespoons bread flour
¼ cup hot water
2 apples, pared and grated
1 egg white

Mix grated rind of Sunkist lemon, Sunkist lemon juice, sugar, egg yolk, slightly beaten, melted butter, bread flour, and hot water. Then add apples which have been pared and grated. When well mixed, fold in stiffly-beaten egg white. Line pie-plates with plain paste, fill with lemon mixture, cover with pastry, and bake.

Orange Shortcake

2 cups bread-flour
6 teaspoons baking-powder
1 teaspoon salt
1 tablespoon sugar
6 tablespoons butter
2 egg yolks
Milk
Sunkist oranges

Mix flour, baking-powder, salt and sugar, and sift together four times. Work in butter, using tips of the fingers. Beat egg yolks; add milk to make three-fourths of a cup; stir into flour, mixing with a knife. Put on board, knead slightly, roll, cut out with a large biscuit-cutter, and bake in a hot oven. Split shortcakes, butter generously, fill with oranges that have been pared, cut in thin sections and sweetened. Serve with whipped cream, marshmallow cream, or ice-cream.

Orange and Raspberry Shortcake

Make shortcake as for Orange Shortcake. Pare four Sunkist oranges; remove sections from membrane; cut each section in three pieces and sprinkle with sugar. Split shortcake, spread generously with butter, then with raspberry jam; cover with oranges; put top of shortcake on; cover with whipped cream, and serve.

Sunkist Shortcake Sauce

4 Sunkist oranges
½ cup sugar
Orange juice
2 tablespoons butter
2 teaspoons arrowroot

Pare oranges, remove sections from membrane, cut in two pieces; add sugar, and let stand one hour. Drain juice; add enough more orange juice to make one cup, and pour over butter and arrowroot, creamed together. Cook, stirring constantly, until thickened; remove from fire, and add orange sections. Split and butter individual shortcakes; put orange sauce between and on top, and serve hot.

Sunkist Recipes

Birch Island Steamed Pudding

2 slices bread
1 tablespoon butter
5 tablespoons Sunkist orange marmalade
1 cup scalded milk
1 tablespoon sugar
½ teaspoon salt
2 eggs

Cut two slices of bread one-half inch thick; remove crusts; cut each slice into four triangular-shaped pieces; spread with butter, then with Sunkist orange marmalade, and line buttered melon mold with pieces. Beat eggs; add sugar, salt, and scalded milk, slowly, while stirring constantly; then pour mixture over the bread. Steam three hours, and serve hot with cream.

Orange Charlotte

1 tablespoon gelatine
¼ cup cold water
¼ cup boiling water
½ cup sugar
1½ cups strained Sunkist orange juice
½ tablespoon Sunkist lemon juice
1½ cups heavy cream
Lady-fingers

Soak gelatine for five minutes in cold water; dissolve in boiling water, and add strained Sunkist orange and lemon juice and sugar. Set dish containing mixture in a pan of crushed ice, and stir until it begins to thicken. Fold in cream, beaten until stiff; line mold with lady-fingers; pour mixture into the centre, and set on ice to stiffen.

Cocoanut Bread Pudding

To Orange Bread Pudding add one-half cup desiccated cocoanut, and sprinkle meringue with cocoanut before baking.

Orange Tapioca Pudding

¼ cup quick cooking tapioca
2 cups milk
2 eggs
½ cup sugar
½ teaspoon salt
3 Sunkist oranges
2 tablespoons sugar

Put milk and tapioca in double boiler; cook fifteen minutes; then add eggs, beaten with salt and one-half cup sugar. Pare oranges; remove sections from membrane; put in bottom of baking-dish; sprinkle with two tablespoons sugar; pour tapioca mixture over oranges, and bake in moderate oven until custard is firm.

Lemon Crumb Pudding

2 cups scalded milk
2 cups bread crumbs
¼ teaspoon salt
¼ cup sugar
1 egg
Grated rind 1 Sunkist lemon
3 tablespoons Sunkist lemon juice
1 tablespoon melted butter

Pour the scalded milk over the fine, dry bread crumbs; add salt and sugar, egg well beaten, grated Sunkist lemon rind, Sunkist lemon juice, and melted butter. Pour into a buttered pudding-dish, and bake in a slow oven forty minutes. Serve with Creamy Lemon Sauce (see page 50).

Orange Bread Pudding

1 cup bread crumbs
2 tablespoons butter
2 cups scalded milk
2 egg yolks
⅓ cup sugar
Juice 2 Sunkist oranges
Grated rind 2 Sunkist oranges

Sunkist Recipes

Soak bread crumbs, butter and scalded milk thirty minutes; then add egg yolks, beaten with sugar, and Sunkist orange juice and rind. Pour into a buttered pudding-dish, and bake in a moderate oven until firm. Cover with Eight-Minute Meringue (see page 49).

Orange Panache

1 tablespoon gelatine
2 tablespoons cold water
2 tablespoons boiling water
2 bananas
1 Sunkist orange
½ Sunkist lemon
½ cup powdered sugar
Few grains salt
1 cup cream

Soak gelatine in cold water; dissolve in hot water. Peel and scrape bananas, and force through a sieve; add pulp and juice of Sunkist orange and Sunkist lemon, sugar, salt, and dissolved gelatine. Set bowl containing mixture in pan of ice-water, stirring occasionally, and when beginning to stiffen, fold in whipped cream. Line fancy mold with slices of "Orange Jelly Roll" (see page 37). Pour in gelatine mixture, and chill. Unmold on glass plate for serving.

Georgette Pudding Sauce

2 eggs
2½ tablespoons sugar
Juice ½ Sunkist lemon
1 tablespoon water
Grated rind ½ Sunkist lemon

Beat yolks of eggs until thick and lemon-colored, beat in one and one-half tablespoons sugar, add Sunkist lemon juice and rind and boiling water, and cook in double boiler, stirring constantly, until thick and creamy. Beat whites of eggs until light; then beat in gradually the remaining sugar. Combine mixtures; cook one minute; stir occasionally until cool; use on cottage pudding, or serve as a dessert in small glasses, lined with lady-fingers or thin slices of sponge cake.

Orange Puff Sauce

2 egg whites
Few grains salt
⅔ cup powdered sugar
1 Sunkist orange
½ Sunkist lemon

Beat whites of eggs and salt until very stiff; add sugar slowly, beating constantly; then add grated rind and juice of the orange and juice of the lemon.

Sunkist Orange Panache

Sunkist Recipes

Orange Syrup Sauce

1 cup Sunkist orange juice
1 teaspoon grated Sunkist orange rind
1 cup sugar
Juice 1 Sunkist lemon
Grated rind ½ Sunkist lemon

Put ingredients into saucepan, and boil fifteen minutes. Skim, strain and pour into sterilized glasses. Use as a sauce on vanilla ice-cream or on baked rice pudding. This sauce, when sealed in sterile glass, will keep well, and will be found convenient to have on hand for emergency in the summer.

Economy Pudding Sauce

1 tablespoon cornstarch
Few gratings Sunkist lemon rind
½ cup sugar
1 cup boiling water
2 tablespoons butter
2 tablespoons Sunkist lemon juice
Few gratings nutmeg
Few grains salt

Mix cornstarch, Sunkist lemon rind and sugar; add water, gradually, stirring constantly, and boil five minutes. Remove from fire; add Sunkist lemon juice, butter and seasonings.

Lemon Tapioca Sherbet Without Freezing

½ cup quick-cooking tapioca
1 cup sugar
2 cups water
Juice 2 Sunkist lemons
2 egg whites

Put tapioca, sugar and water into double boiler, and cook, stirring often, until clear. Three minutes before removing from fire, add Sunkist lemon juice. When cool and beginning to thicken, add the stiffly-beaten egg whites, and beat well. Serve with boiled custard or heavy cream.

Orange Fairy Fluff

4 egg yolks
4 tablespoons sugar
¾ cup Sunkist orange juice
Grated rind 1 Sunkist orange
Grated rind 1 Sunkist lemon
Juice 1 Sunkist lemon
2 tablespoons hot water
4 egg whites
2 tablespoons sugar
Lady-fingers

Beat egg yolks with four tablespoons sugar; add Sunkist orange juice and grated rind, Sunkist lemon juice and grated rind, and hot water, and cook in double boiler until mixture thickens, stirring constantly. Beat egg whites until stiff, add two tablespoons sugar, and fold into first mixture. Chill; line sherbet glasses with lady-fingers; fill with orange mixture, and serve.

Hampshire Fruit Pudding

1 cup suet
1 cup chopped raw carrot
2⅔ cups stale bread crumbs
4 egg yolks
1⅓ cups brown sugar
Grated rind 1 Sunkist lemon
1 tablespoon Sunkist lemon juice
½ chopped candied Sunkist orange peel
¾ cup raisins
½ cup currants
2 tablespoons flour
1½ teaspoons salt
1 teaspoon cinnamon
½ teaspoon grated nutmeg
¼ teaspoon cloves
4 egg whites

Put suet and carrot twice through the meat-grinder; then work until creamy, and add bread crumbs. Beat egg yolks until light, and add sugar, gradually, while beating

Sunkist Recipes

constantly. Combine mixtures and add Sunkist lemon rind and juice. Mix chopped Sunkist orange peel, raisins, cut in pieces, and currants, and dredge with flour, mixed and sifted with salt and spices. Add to mixture with whites of eggs, beaten until stiff. Turn into a buttered mold, garnished with Sunkist orange peel, cut in fancy shapes; adjust cover, and steam three and one-half hours.

Iced Orange Sauce

Peel of 2 Sunkist oranges
¼ cup sugar
½ cup water
1 teaspoon gelatine
1 tablespoon cold water
Juice 2 Sunkist oranges
1 tablespoon Maraschino syrup
¼ teaspoon vanilla

Cut the thin yellow peel of two Sunkist oranges in fine threads; boil in water five minutes, and drain. Boil sugar with one-half cup water five minutes; add gelatine, soaked in one tablespoon cold water; then add Sunkist orange juice and Maraschino syrup, and strain. Add the shredded Sunkist orange peel and vanilla, and serve ice cold.

Lemon Syrup Sauce

1 cup sugar
⅓ cup water
1 tablespoon butter
1½ tablespoons Sunkist lemon juice

Make a syrup by boiling water and sugar for eight minutes; remove from fire; add butter and Sunkist lemon juice; strain, and serve with fritters or simple puddings.

Orange Puffs

1¼ cups flour
2 teaspoons baking-powder
½ cup sugar
¼ teaspoon salt
½ cup milk
1 egg
1 tablespoon butter
½ teaspoon grated Sunkist orange rind

Sift flour, baking-powder, sugar and salt into mixing-bowl; add milk, gradually, egg, well beaten, melted butter, and orange rind. Beat two minutes; pour into greased muffin-pans, and bake twenty to thirty minutes in moderate oven. Serve with Orange Sauce (see page 45).

Lemon Syrup

1 cup sugar syrup
⅔ cup Sunkist lemon juice

Mix sugar syrup and lemon juice; strain, bottle, and keep in the refrigerator. When wanted, dilute with six parts ice-water to one part lemon syrup, and serve from a glass pitcher, garnishing, if desired, with thin slices of Sunkist lemon or orange, Maraschino cherries, or sprigs of mint. Lemon syrup is convenient to take for picnics or in the automobile lunch-basket.

Bride's Cake

Sunkist Recipes

Sugar Syrup

2 cups sugar
2 cups water

Put sugar and water in saucepan; stir until sugar is dissolved; boil five minutes; cool, and bottle. The syrup may be kept in the refrigerator, and will be found much more satisfactory than sugar for sweetening lemon and orangeades and fruit beverages.

Sherbet Fizz

Orange ice
1 egg white
Fresh mint
Ginger ale

Make orange ice, and freeze to a mush. Add egg white, beaten stiff, and continue freezing until firm. Wipe mint leaves dry; chop; put sherbet in individual glasses; sprinkle with mint, and fill glasses with ginger ale. Cold tea may be used in place of ginger ale.

Fresh Mint Sherbet

4 cups water
2 cups sugar
1 cup Sunkist lemon juice
1 bunch fresh mint

Boil water and sugar five minutes. Add lemon juice, and strain mixture over the finely-cut leaves from the bunch of mint. Let stand until cold, freeze, and serve, instead of mint jelly, with hot roast of lamb.

Lemon Cocoanut Cream

Juice ½ Sunkist lemon
Grated rind 1 Sunkist lemon
½ cup powdered sugar
1 egg yolk
½ cup shredded cocoanut

Put Sunkist lemon juice and rind, and sugar, in a double boiler, and add egg yolks slightly beaten. Cook ten minutes stirring constantly, then add cocoanut. Cool, and use as a filling for light cake.

Spun Sugar

2 cups sugar
1 cup water
1 teaspoon Sunkist lemon juice

Boil sugar, water, Sunkist lemon juice, and color paste, as desired, without stirring, to 300° or until it just begins to change color. Place saucepan at once in cold water, and when boiling ceases, in hot water. Dip fork, or bunch of wires, in syrup, and shake swiftly back and forth between two rods. Gather it up and place on cool platter. Use for decoration around frozen desserts.

Candy roses. Boil ingredients, as for Spun Sugar, to 300°; pour onto a buttered pan; keep near warm oven, and pull a small portion at a time, until glossy. Stretch and pull into shape of rose petals, fastening petals at base with drops of melted candy. Shape leaves from dark green candy.

Orange Frosting

Grated rind 1 Sunkist orange
3 tablespoons Sunkist orange juice
1 teaspoon Sunkist lemon juice
1 egg yolk
Confectioners' sugar

Mix grated Sunkist orange rind with fruit juices and let stand fifteen minutes. Strain into egg yolk, beaten until thick and lemon-colored, and add sifted confectioners' sugar until of right consistency to spread.

Sunkist Recipes

Orange Syrup

Rind of 1 Sunkist orange
2 cups water
3 cups sugar
9 Sunkist oranges
4 Sunkist lemons

Pare off yellow rind of Sunkist orange, and boil with sugar and water ten minutes; strain, and when cool, add juice of Sunkist oranges and lemons. Use with twice as much ice-water for plain punch or orangeade. It may be kept in the refrigerator, and used as desired.

Pineapple Cocktail

1 pineapple
1 cup sugar
⅓ cup water
½ cup Sunkist orange juice
⅓ cup grapefruit juice
Pink color paste

Boil sugar and water three minutes; cool; add fruit juices, and color a delicate pink. Cut fresh pineapple cylinders, using an apple-corer, and cut cylinders into half-inch lengths. Put in glasses, and cover with syrup.

Orange Harlequin

2 cups Sunkist blood orange juice
⅓ cup Sunkist lemon juice
1 cup sugar
1 cup heavy cream
½ cup powdered sugar
½ tablespoon vanilla
Few grains salt
⅔ cup nut meats

Mix fruit juices and sugar, and strain mixture into a one-quart ice-cream mold. Whip cream; add powdered sugar, vanilla, salt, and nut meats, cut in fine pieces, and pour over the first mixture until mold is full to overflowing. Cover with buttered paper, then with cover of mold; pack in ice and salt, using two parts ice to one part salt, and let stand three hours. Un-mold, and cut in slices for serving. Dried macaroon crumbs may be used in place of nut meats.

Eight-Minute Meringue

3 egg whites
½ cup powdered sugar (scant)
Grated rind Sunkist orange or lemon

Beat egg whites with Dover egg-beater until stiff, gradually add two-thirds the sugar beating vigorously, fold in remaining sugar; add grated Sunkist lemon rind to flavor, and bake eight minutes in a moderate oven.

Mocha Cakes

Cut slices from Orange Jelly Roll, or little shapes from a sheet of fine-grained cake. Frost sides with Orange Butter Frosting, and roll in shredded cocoanut. Then frost tops, and decorate with frosting, colored, if desired, and forced through pastry-bags, made of strong paper. The ends of the cone-shaped bags may be cut to leave a small opening through which the frosting is forced, making letters, or conventional designs.

Little Mocha Cakes

Sunkist Recipes

Creamy Lemon Sauce
¼ cup butter
½ cup powdered sugar
Grated rind ½ Sunkist lemon
1 tablespoon Sunkist lemon juice

Cream the butter; add sugar, gradually, while beating constantly; then add grated Sunkist lemon rind, and Sunkist lemon juice, drop by drop.

If desired, this sauce may be warmed over hot water, beaten thoroughly, and used as a liquid sauce.

Baked Orange Custard
3 egg yolks
1 egg white
½ cup sugar
Few grains salt
Grated rind 1 Sunkist orange
¼ cup Sunkist orange juice
1¼ cups milk

Beat yolks and white of egg until light; add sugar, salt, grated Sunkist orange rind and Sunkist orange juice. Scald milk in double boiler; pour gradually, while stirring constantly, over egg mixture; pour into buttered custard cups, placed in a pan of hot water, and bake in a moderate oven until custard becomes firm. Cool, and serve with whipped cream on top, or turn out and surround with sections of orange and orange syrup.

Orange Cream Custard
6 tablespoons sugar
Grated rind ⅓ Sunkist orange
Juice 2 Sunkist oranges
2 egg yolks
1 cup cream
Whipped cream

Dissolve sugar in Sunkist orange juice; add Sunkist orange rind, egg yolks well beaten, and cream, and cook in double boiler, stirring constantly, until it begins to thicken. Chill and serve in glass cups, with whipped cream. The beaten white of two eggs can be used in place of whipped cream, if desired.

Tulip Dessert
4 small Sunkist oranges
½ cup white grapes
½ cup nut meats
1 cup scalded milk
¼ cup sugar
1 egg yolk
1 tablespoon cornstarch

Cut the top from an orange, and remove pulp. Cut orange into four segments; shape, and bend outward a little, to simulate a tulip. Mix cornstarch and sugar, and stir into hot milk. Cook ten minutes, stirring occasionally. Pour onto well-beaten egg yolk; return to double boiler, and cook one minute; then cool. Mix with orange pulp, grapes, seeded and skinned, and nut meats. Fill orange skins, and serve in long-stemmed sherbet glasses; garnish with fresh green leaves.

Sunkist Strawberries
1 box strawberries
Juice 2 Sunkist oranges
1 cup sugar
½ cup heavy cream
2 tablespoons powdered sugar
¼ teaspoon vanilla

Wash and hull strawberries; cover with Sunkist orange juice, mixed with one cup sugar, and chill thoroughly. Serve in champagne glasses. Beat the cream until stiff. Add powdered sugar and vanilla, and, with the pastry-bag and tube, pipe a border around each glass.

Sunkist Recipes

Puff-Ball Oranges

1 egg white
½ cup powdered sugar
4 Sunkist oranges

Peel small Sunkist oranges, removing white membrane with outer skin. Beat egg white, slightly, using wire whisk; add sugar, gradually, and continue beating until meringue is stiff and will hold its shape. Thrust a long, slender wire skewer through the centre of each orange; frost them completely with the meringue, and suspend them, by the skewers, across a narrow pan, and bake twelve minutes in a slow oven, being careful not to let them brown. Twist skewers gently to remove them. These oranges make a pretty dessert or supper dish.

Lemon Mincemeat

4 Sunkist lemons
4 apples
1 pound currants
1¾ cups sugar
½ cup nuts
½ cup raisins
Cinnamon ⎫
Ginger ⎪
Nutmeg ⎬ 1 teaspoon each
Allspice ⎪
Cloves ⎪
Salt ⎭
½ cup butter

Squeeze juice from Sunkist lemons, and cook peel until soft, changing the water twice. Put through meat-chopper, and then rub through a sieve. Chop apples, add Sunkist lemon peel and juice and remaining ingredients, mix well and store in jars. Use as a filling for turnovers or pies.

Orange Caramel

6 Sunkist oranges
½ cup sugar
½ cup water
½ cup cream
Pistachio nuts

Pare Sunkist oranges, removing membrane with peel, and cut crosswise, in slices. Put sugar and water in a small saucepan, and boil, quickly, until sugar is a golden brown. Arrange layer of Sunkist orange slices in glass dish; sprinkle with sugar; pour over enough caramel syrup to form a thin coating over the orange; add another layer of orange and caramel; repeat until orange is used. Beat cream until stiff, pile lightly on the orange, and sprinkle with chopped pistachio nuts.

Boiled Orange Frosting

1 cup sugar
⅓ cup Sunkist orange juice
Grated rind 1 Sunkist orange
1 egg white

In a smooth agate saucepan put sugar and Sunkist orange juice and rind, mix well, and boil, being careful not to stir or disturb syrup until it will spin a long thread when it drips from tip of spoon. Lift gently from fire, and pour slowly, while beating vigorously with a strong egg-beater, in a fine stream onto egg white which has been beaten until light but not stiff. Continue beating until frosting is stiff enough to stay in place, pour all at once onto cake and spread over surface with a few movements of a large, flat knife.

Sunkist Recipes

Orange Butter Frosting

4 tablespoons Sunkist orange juice
1 teaspoon grated Sunkist orange rind
⅓ cup butter
1 cup powdered sugar

Mix Sunkist orange juice and rind; let stand one-half hour, and strain through cheesecloth. Cream butter in a warm, but not hot, bowl. Add sugar gradually, and beat until light. Let Sunkist orange juice get slightly warm and add drop by drop to first mixture. This may be used for frosting large or small cakes. Portions may be colored and used through paper frosting-bags for decorations. The cake should be kept in a cool place until required.

This frosting may be used as a pudding sauce.

Tartlet Shells, or Baskets

Cover the outside of individual scalloped tins with pastry, pricking several times with a fork, and bake in a moderate oven. Remove from tins, and fill as desired. Or, line tins with pastry, then with paraffin paper, and fill with raw rice or beans. Bake in moderate oven; remove filling and paper, and use as desired. Handles may be made from strips of pastry, twisted and baked over a baking-powder box, then removed, and kept upright in tartlet shell by the filling used.

Cream Pie Crust

1 cup flour
⅓ teaspoon baking-powder
⅓ teaspoon salt
⅓ cup heavy cream
2 tablespoons butter

Sift together flour, baking-powder and salt; add heavy cream to moisten; put on floured board, knead slightly, roll thin, spread with butter well creamed, fold over, roll out again, line pie-plate, put in filling, and bake.

Frozen Oranges, Whole

For breakfast or luncheon, on a hot day, cover Sunkist oranges with ice and salt, using three parts of finely-crushed ice and one part rock salt, and leave one to two hours. Remove, rinse, cut in halves, and serve, sprinkled with powdered sugar.

Orange Granite

2 cups Sunkist orange pulp
½ cup sugar
2 tablespoons Sunkist lemon juice

Pare oranges, removing white membrane with peel; cut in small pieces; add sugar and Sunkist lemon juice, and freeze, using one part salt to three parts ice in freezing. May be served with meat course, if desired.

Lemon Ice

3 cups water
1⅓ cups sugar
½ cup Sunkist lemon juice

Boil sugar and water five minutes; add lemon juice; cool, and strain into freezer. Pack with three parts ice to one part salt; let stand five minutes, then freeze until stiff. Remove dasher, pack mixture down into freezer, drain off salt water, repack freezer with four parts ice and one part salt, and leave to ripen until needed.

Sunkist Recipes

Sunkist Orange Ice-Cream

Lemaschino Bombe

Line a melon mold with lemon ice; fill with Maraschino Cream; cover with lemon ice, and proceed as with Bombe Glace. Garnish with Maraschino Cream, forced through pastry-bag and tube, candied lemon peel and candied cherries.

Maraschino Cream. Beat two cups heavy cream until stiff; add one-half cup powdered sugar, two tablespoons Maraschino Cordial, and a few grains salt.

Bombe Glace

Line a mold with orange ice, made, if convenient, with blood oranges. Fill centre with whipped cream, sweetened and flavored with vanilla; cover with orange ice, then with buttered paper, buttered side up; then with tight tin cover. Pack in two parts crushed ice, mixed with one part rock salt, and let stand three hours. Unmold, and garnish, if desired, with spun sugar and candy roses.

Orange Ice

2 cups water
1 cup sugar
⅓ cup Sunkist lemon juice
1 cup Sunkist orange juice
Few gratings Sunkist orange rind

Boil water, sugar and Sunkist orange rind five minutes; cool; add Sunkist lemon and orange juice; strain, and freeze, following directions for Lemon Ice.

Honey Mousse

2 Sunkist oranges
1 teaspoon granulated gelatine
1 tablespoon cold water
1 cup strained honey
2 cups heavy cream

Peel Sunkist oranges, removing inner membrane with rind, and cut in small pieces. Soak gelatine in cold water; heat the honey; add gelatine, stirring until dissolved; add orange; remove from fire, and when cold, add cream, beaten stiff. Put in mold; pack in equal parts ice and salt, and let stand three or four hours.

Sunkist Recipes

Sunkist Sundae

Put a large spoonful of Orange Sauce, colored red, or made with Sunkist blood oranges, in bottom of a long-stemmed glass, and add a spoonful of vanilla ice-cream. Make a depression in the ice-cream, and put there a spoonful of fresh or preserved fruit; cover with ice-cream, then with heavy cream, beaten stiff. Over all pour more Orange Sauce, and serve at once.

Fruit Milk Sherbet

3 Sunkist lemons
1 cup sugar
2 small bananas
1½ peaches
2 cups milk
1 cup chopped nuts

Squeeze the lemons and strain juice into the sugar; add other fruit pulp, rubbed through a sieve; then add milk and nuts, and freeze as usual. Serve with Iced Orange Sauce.

Orange Cream Sherbet

Grated rind 1 Sunkist orange
2 cups boiling water
1 cup sugar
1 cup Sunkist orange juice
Juice 2 Sunkist lemons
1½ cups heavy cream
½ cup sugar

Pour boiling water over rind; add one cup sugar; cover closely, and let stand one-half hour; strain; add orange and lemon juice. Freeze to a mush; add cream, beaten until stiff and sweetened with one-half cup sugar, and finish freezing.

Blood Orange Ice-Cream

1 cup heavy cream
Sugar
2 cups Sunkist blood orange juice

Add cream, slowly, to orange juice, and sweeten to taste. Freeze like lemon ice. Serve with fresh or canned strawberries, with marshmallow cream, or with spun sugar and candy roses.

Sunkist Coupe

1 Sunkist orange
1 banana
2 teaspoons Maraschino syrup
Maraschino cherries
1 slice pineapple
1 teaspoon Sunkist lemon juice
Few grains salt
Orange or Lemon Ice
Powdered sugar

Mix the pulp of the Sunkist orange with pineapple and banana, cut in small pieces; add lemon juice, Maraschino syrup, salt, and powdered sugar, to taste. Fill champagne glasses two-thirds full of fruit, cover with Orange or Lemon Ice, and garnish with cherries.

Two-in-One Sherbet

2 cups sugar
2 cups water
2 Sunkist oranges
2 Sunkist lemons
1 pineapple
2 bananas
2 egg whites

Boil sugar and water five minutes; cool; add pulp and juice of oranges, juice of lemons, pineapple, chopped fine, and bananas, rubbed through a sieve. Freeze to a mush; add egg whites, beaten stiff, and finish freezing.

Lemon Milk Sherbet

Juice of 3 Sunkist lemons
1½ cups sugar
3 cups of milk
1 cup cream

Sunkist Recipes

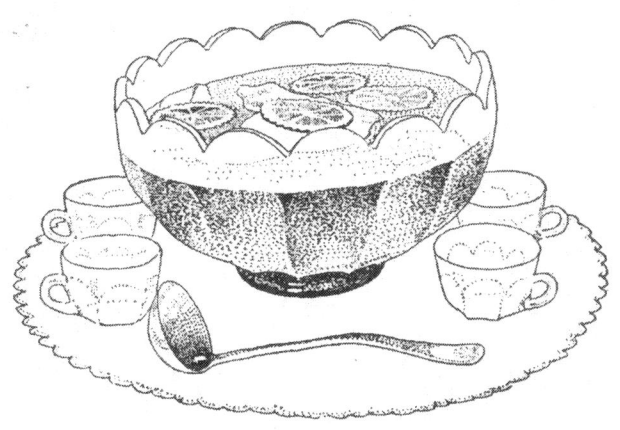

Sunkist Orange Punch

Mix Sunkist lemon juice and sugar, and add milk and cream, gradually. Freeze, following directions for freezing given under Lemon Ice.

Milk or sour cream, in which has been dissolved one-half teaspoon soda, may be used in place of sweet cream.

Cardinal Punch

1 pint cranberries
1 pint water
½ cup Sunkist orange juice
1½ tablespoons Sunkist lemon juice
1 cup sugar syrup
1 pint soda water or Apollinaris

Cook cranberries and water until fruit is very soft; then strain through a double thickness of cheesecloth. When cool, add fruit juices, syrup and charged water; pour over a block of ice, or a mold of frozen orange or lemon ice.

Ginger Ale Punch

1 cup sugar
1 cup hot tea infusion
¾ cup Sunkist orange juice
⅓ cup Sunkist lemon juice
1 pint ginger ale
1 pint Apollinaris
Few slices Sunkist orange

Pour tea over sugar, and, as soon as sugar is dissolved, add fruit juices; strain into punch-bowl over a large piece of ice, and, just before serving, add ginger ale, Apollinaris, and slices of Sunkist orange.

Lemonade

Juice 1 Sunkist lemon
2 tablespoons sugar
¾ cup water

Put sugar in cup; add icewater; stir until sugar is dissolved; add Sunkist lemon juice, and serve immediately. Soda water, Apollinaris water, or boiling water may be used if desired.

Sunkist Recipes

Oriental Punch

1 cup sugar syrup
6 cloves
1-inch stick cinnamon
1 tablespoon chopped Canton ginger
Juice of 2 Sunkist lemons
Juice of 3 Sunkist oranges
1 drop oil of peppermint
Green coloring
Fresh mint leaves

Add cloves, cinnamon and Canton ginger to hot syrup; cover, and let stand until cold. Add fruit juices, coloring, and peppermint; strain over a piece of ice, and garnish with fresh mint leaves.

Nutritious Lemonade

3 tablespoons milk sugar
½ cup boiling water
2 tablespoons Sunkist lemon juice
¼ cup crushed ice

Add milk sugar to boiling water, and boil until sugar is dissolved. Cool, and add to lemon juice and crushed ice. More sugar may be used, if desired, to increase the food value.

Fig Lemonade

4 figs
2 cups water
½ tablespoon sea-moss farina
⅓ cup sugar
3 tablespoons Sunkist lemon juice
Grated rind of 1 Sunkist lemon

Chop figs fine; add remaining ingredients, and simmer forty-five minutes; strain and cool. This is soothing to an irritated throat, and will sometimes relieve a cough. One-half cup Irish moss, soaked three minutes in cold water, and drained, may be used instead of sea-moss farina.

Egg Lemonade

1 egg
2 tablespoons powdered sugar
2 tablespoons Sunkist lemon juice
2 tablespoons crushed ice
¼ cup cold water

Beat egg and powdered sugar; add water and lemon juice, and strain over crushed ice.

Mint Cup

3 Sunkist lemons
1 bunch mint
½ cup sugar syrup
½ cup water
1 pint ginger ale

Remove leaves from two-thirds of the sprigs of mint and bruise with the fingers; add Sunkist lemon juice and syrup, and let stand one-half hour. Strain over piece of ice, and add ginger ale. Garnish with tips from remaining sprigs of mint.

Grape Juice Punch

To Mint Cup (see above), add one cup grape juice and one Sunkist lemon, cut in very thin slices.

Afternoon Tea

3 teaspoons tea
Sunkist lemon slices
Cloves
Orange loaf-sugar
2 cups boiling water
Candied cherries
Sunkist orange marmalade
Sunkist lemon loaf-sugar

Sunkist Recipes

Iced Tea

Have water freshly boiling, and pour over tea in a scalded teapot, or over teaball, or perforated double teaspoon, in china cup. Let stand only long enough to become the right strength, but never more than five minutes. With orange pekoe tea, less than one minute infusion is sufficient. Serve at once with thin slices of Sunkist lemon, a clove, a cherry, and sugar, to taste; or, sweeten with Sunkist orange marmalade, or orange or lemon loaf-sugar.

Lemon Albumen

1 egg white
½ cup cold water
Sunkist lemon juice

Stir white of egg and water with silver fork, or cut with knife and fork, until albumen is completely dissolved; add lemon juice, to make palatable; strain, and use in sickness, as ordered.

Iced Tea

4 teaspoons tea
2 cups boiling water
Sunkist lemons

Pour boiling water over tea; let stand five minutes, and strain into glasses half full of crushed ice. Allow one or two slices of Sunkist lemon and sugar, to taste, for each glass; or, add one teaspoon Sunkist lemon juice to each glass, and place slice of lemon on edge of glass.

Lemon Whey

½ cup milk
4 teaspoons Sunkist lemon juice

Add lemon juice to milk, and let stand five minutes; strain through a double thickness of cheesecloth. The Whey is used by invalids when milk cannot be taken.

The curds can be seasoned with salt, paprika, and butter, and used as a sandwich filling.

Sunkist Recipes

Orange Egg-Nog

1 egg
1 tablespoon sugar
⅛ teaspoon salt
Juice of 1 Sunkist orange
Juice of ½ Sunkist lemon
¼ cup crushed ice

Beat white of egg until stiff; add, gradually, one-half the sugar and salt, and one-half the Sunkist orange juice. To yolk of egg add remaining sugar and fruit juices, and beat until thick. Put ice in glass; pour in first mixture; then gently fold in second mixture, and serve.

Camino Fruit Cup

¼ cup Sunkist lemon juice
½ cup Sunkist orange juice
½ cup sugar syrup
1 cup pineapple syrup
2 cups ice-water

Mix ingredients, using syrup drained from can of pineapple, and strain over a piece of ice. Serve in high, narrow tumblers which have been frosted by dipping the edges quickly into lemon juice and then in coarse sugar. Place a small slice of canned pineapple on top and a sprig of mint and two straws in the centre, where hollowed out; add a large cherry or strawberry, and serve.

Orange Albumen

1 egg white
⅓ cup Sunkist orange juice
2 tablespoons crushed ice
Sugar syrup

Stir white of egg, using silver fork; add, gradually, orange juice, and strain over crushed ice; then add sugar syrup, if necessary.

Sunkist Recipes

Breakfast and Miscellaneous

Griddle Cakes

2 cups flour
1 tablespoon baking-powder
1 teaspoon salt
3 tablespoons sugar
1½ cups milk
1 egg
3 tablespoons melted butter
Orange marmalade

Mix and sift dry ingredients; add beaten egg and milk; beat thoroughly, and add butter. Drop, by large spoonfuls, on a hot griddle that has been rubbed over with a piece of raw turnip, which will prevent cakes from sticking without the use of butter or grease. When griddle-cake is puffed, full of bubbles, and cooked on edges, turn, and cook on other side. Spread cakes with Sunkist orange marmalade; roll up like jelly-rolls; sprinkle with sugar, and serve at once.

Bran Muffins

½ cup flour
½ teaspoon salt
1 cup bran
¾ cup Sunkist orange juice
½ teaspoon soda
1½ tablespoons molasses
2 tablespoons melted butter

Sift flour and salt; add bran, Sunkist orange juice (in which soda has been dissolved and stirred until it begins to froth), molasses, and melted butter. Beat vigorously, and pour quickly into hot, buttered gem-pans, and bake in a hot oven.

Marmalade French Toast

2 eggs
½ teaspoon salt
1 tablespoon sugar
1 cup milk
6 slices bread ⅓-inch thick
Sunkist orange marmalade

Sunkist Recipes

Sunkist Orange Sections

Beat eggs; add salt, sugar and milk. Spread bread with Sunkist orange marmalade; put slices together in pairs; soak in egg and milk mixture until softened, and cook on a hot, buttered griddle until delicately browned; turn, and brown on other side, and serve for breakfast or lunch.

Orange Toast

1 teaspoon cornstarch
1 tablespoon cold water
Juice 1 Sunkist orange
¼ cup Sunkist orange pulp
Few grains salt
Sugar
Cinnamon

Mix cornstarch and cold water; add Sunkist orange juice, and boil, stirring constantly for five minutes. Add Sunkist orange pulp and salt, pour over buttered toast, and sprinkle with sugar and cinnamon.

Oranges for Breakfast

1. Use large Sunkist oranges; cut in two, crosswise; loosen pulp from skin with a grapefruit knife, and remove membrane. Serve one-half on each fruit-plate, with an orange-spoon. Garnish with green leaves and a candied cherry. The edge of the peel may be cut in small points if desired.

2. Pare Sunkist oranges and remove sections free from membrane. Make a cone of paper one and one-half inches high, pointed at one end, and one inch in diameter at the other end. Sift some powdered sugar; pack solidly into the cone; turn out onto the middle of a fruit-plate, and arrange sections radiating from the base.

3. Remove sections from a large Sunkist orange and a small grapefruit, free from membrane, and arrange, alternately, around a mound of sugar.

4. Cut Sunkist oranges in two; remove pulp with an orange-spoon, and serve in a small glass.

Sunkist Recipes

5. Make two cuts through a Sunkist orange skin, and remove peel, leaving a band one-half inch wide around the middle of the orange. Cut band and open orange, separating the sections. Arrange on a plate, with a mound of powdered sugar.

Baked Orange for a Cold

Cut a slice, not quite through, for a lid, across the top of a Sunkist orange. With a sharp French knife remove the core, put in a teaspoon, each, of orange syrup and lime juice; bake until heated through; place a cream peppermint candy in the centre, and serve.

Graham Muffins

½ *cup flour*
½ *teaspoon salt*
2 *tablespoons sugar*
¾ *cup Graham flour*
Grated rind ½ *Sunkist orange*
⅛ *cup Sunkist orange juice*
½ *teaspoon soda*
2 *tablespoons shortening*

Sift flour, salt and sugar; add Graham flour, grated rind of Sunkist orange, Sunkist orange juice (in which soda is dissolved and stirred until it begins to get frothy), and melted shortening. Beat well, and pour quickly into hot, buttered muffin-pans, and bake.

A Suggestion for Breakfast

Sunkist Recipes

Index

Meats and Fish *13-31*
Sauces and Relishes *13-31*
Jellies and Vegetables *13-31*
Breads and Sandwiches *13-31*
Salads and Dressings *32-58*
Desserts and Beverages *32-58*
Breakfast and Miscellaneous *59-61*

Ada's Lemon Pie	43	Desserts and Beverages	32-58
Afternoon Tea	56	Devil's Food	38
Arlington Asparagus	28	Dinner—	
Artichokes, Italian Style	28	Meats and Fish	13-31
Baked Orange, for a Cold	61	Sauces and Relishes	13-31
Baked Orange Custard	50	Jellies and Vegetables	13-31
Banana Canoes	22	Breads and Sandwiches	13-31
Beet Relish	29	Economy Pudding Sauce	46
Birch Island Steamed Pudding	44	Egg Lemonade	56
Blood Orange Ice-Cream	54	Egg Sauce	17
Boiled Salad Dressing	35	Eight-Minute Meringue	49
Boiled Fish	14	Fifteen-Dollar Pie	42
Boiled Orange Frosting	51	Fig and Cheese Salad	33
Bombe Glacé	53	Fig Lemonade	66
Bran Muffins	59	Filled Cookies	39
Breakfast and Miscellaneous	59-61	Fillets of Haddock, Lemon Sauce	14
Camino Fruit Cup	58	French Dressing	33
Candied Sunkist Orange Peel	23	French Dressing, with Orange Vinegar	36
Cardinal Punch	55	Fresh Mint Sherbet	48
Carrots and Turnips, Princess	29	Frozen Fruit Salad	34
Cauliflower Mousselaine	29	Frozen Oranges, Whole	52
Caviaré Canapés	16	Fruit Milk Sherbet	54
Chocolate Candied Orange Peel	27	Galantine	15
Citrus Soufflé	40	Genoa Cake	38
Cocoanut Bread Pudding	44	Georgette Pudding Sauce	45
Colonial Sandwiches	31	German Sour Beef	17
Conserve	19	Ginger Ale Fruit Salad	33
Court Bouillon	17	Ginger Ale Punch	55
Cream French Dressing	35	Golden Salad Dressing	34
Cream Mayonnaise Dressing	36	Graham Muffins	61
Cream Pie Crust	52	Grapefruit Marmalade	22
Creamy Lemon Sauce	50		
Cumberland Sauce for Duck	20		

Sunkist Recipes

Grape Juice Punch	56
Griddle Cakes	59
Hampshire Fruit Pudding	46
Hollandaise Sauce	17
Honey Salad Dressing	34
Honey Mousse	53
Horseradish Hollandaise Sauce	18
Iced Orange Sauce	47
Iced Tea	57
Japanese Rice	16
Jellied Oranges, Cut in Sections	25
Jellied Vegetable Salad	33
Lemaschino Bombe	53
Lemonade	55
Lemon Albumen	57
Lemon Bavarian Cream	20
Lemon Butter	23
Lemon Catsup	22
Lemon Cocoanut Cream	48
Lemon Crumb Pudding	44
Lemon Drop Cookies	39
Lemon Extract	26
Lemon Honey	19
Lemon Honey Sandwiches	30
Lemon Ice	52
Lemon Jelly	25
Lemon Loaf Sugar	23
Lemon Milk Sherbet	54
Lemon Mince-Meat	51
Lemon Pectin Extraction	26
Lemon Pie, with Bread Crumbs	42
Lemon Queen Cake	39
Lemon Syrup	47
Lemon Syrup Sauce	47
Lemon Tapioca Sherbet, without Freezing	46
Lemon Whey	57
Little Neck Clams	14
Lobster Cocktail	14
Mackerel, with Lemon Butter	14
Maitre d'Hotel Butter	23
Marmalade French Toast	59
Marshmallow Salad	36
Martinique French Dressing	35
Mayonnaise Dressing	35
Mint Cup	56
Mint Jelly, with Gelatine	25
Mint Jelly, with Orange Pectin	24
Mocha Cakes	49
Mock Hollandaise Sauce	18
Mock Lobster Salad	33
Mousselaine Sauce	17
New York Salad	32
Nutritious Lemonade	56
Orange Albumen	58
Orange Balls	41
Orange Bavarian Cream	20
Orange Bread	30
Orange Bread Pudding	44
Oranges for Breakfast	60
Orange Butter Frosting	52
Orange Cake	40
Orange Cake Filling	40
Orange Caramel	51
Orange Charlotte	44
Orange Cream Custard	50
Orange Cream Sherbet	54
Orange Egg-Nogg	58
Orange Fairy Fluff	46
Orange Filling	41
Orange Fondant	27
Orange Fritters	26
Orange Frosting	48
Orange Fruit Cake	37
Orange Fudge	41
Orange Granite	52
Orange Harlequin	49
Orange Honey Sandwiches	30
Orange Ice	53
Orange Jelly	19
Orange Jelly, without Gelatine	20
Orange Jelly, with Fruit	21
Orange Jelly Roll	37
Orange and Lemon Marmalade	19
Orange Loaf Sugar	23
Orange Marmalade	19
Orange Marmalade Bavarian Cream	18
Orange Mint Sauce for Lamb	20
Orange Panaché	45
Orange and Peanut Salad	32
Orange Pectin Extraction	26
Orange Peel Bread	30
Orange Pie Filling	37
Orange Pin-Wheels	22

Sunkist Recipes

Orange Puffs	47	Rhubarb Jelly	27
Orange Puff Sauce	45	Russian Salad Dressing	36
Orange and Raspberry Shortcake	43	Salmon Chartreuse	15
Orange and Rhubarb Sauce	21	Salads and Dressings	32–58
Orange Roly-Poly	37	Sardines, with Lemon	16
Orange Salad	34	Sauted Tomatoes	29
Orange Shortcake	43	Savory Butter Sandwiches	30
Orange Sponge Cake	38	Scallop Cocktail	13
Orange Straws	27	Sherbet Fizz	48
Orange Sweet Pickle	22	Spinach, with Sunkist Lemon	28
Orange Syrup	49	Spun Sugar	48
Orange Syrup Sauce	46	Star Salad	35
Orange Tapioca Pudding	44	Strawberry Jelly	24
Orange Toast	60	Sugar Syrup	48
Orange Vinegar	20	Sunkist Coupé	54
Oriental Punch	56	Sunkist Lemon Pie	42
Oysters, with Cocktail Sauce	13	Sunkist Shortcake Sauce	43
Oysters on the Half-Shell	13	Sunkist Strawberries	50
Oyster Plant, with Fine Herbs	28	Sunkist Sundae	54
Pastry	39	Sweet Croquettes	26
Peanut Rice Salad	32	Tartlet Shells or Baskets	52
Pepper Butter	23	Thousand Island Salad Dressing	36
Pineapple Cocktail	49	Toasted Marmalade Sandwiches	31
Pineapple Jelly	25	To Remove Pulp from Orange	12
Princess Potatoes	29	Tulip Dessert	50
Princess Sauce	20	Turkish Delight	41
Puff-Ball Oranges	51	Two-in-One Sherbet	54
Rolled Orange Wafers	38		

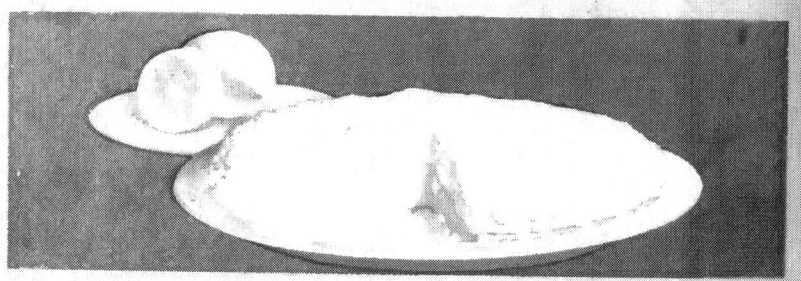

Made in the USA
San Bernardino, CA
18 June 2017